An Operators Manual
for Combat PTSD

◆

An Operators Manual for Combat PTSD

Essays for Coping

Ashley B. Hart II, Ph.D.

Writer's Showcase
presented by *Writer's Digest*
San Jose New York Lincoln Shanghai

An Operators Manual for Combat PTSD
Essays for Coping

Writer's Showcase
presented by *Writer's Digest*
an imprint of iUniverse.com, Inc.

For information address:
iUniverse.com, Inc.
620 North 48th Street, Suite 201
Lincoln, NE 68504-3467
www.iuniverse.com

ISBN: 0-595-13798-9

Printed in the United States of America

In Memory,

Doc Rhino
1/5
17 February, 1968

Epigraph

◆

That makes a man go mad for all his goodness of
reason, a rage that rises within and swirls like
smoke in the heart and becomes in our madness a
thing more sweet than dripping of honey.

Homer,
The Iliad

Contents

———◆———

Epigraph vii

Foreword xiii

Acknowledgements xv

Introduction xvii

Keeping It In The Smart Brain
Utilizing Spreading Activation:
How To Use This Manual 1

PTSD/It's A Stress Disorder/It's
An Anxiety Disorder 6

Awareness Of Thoughts, Feelings,
And Bodily Sensations 7

The Nature And Course Of Trauma 9

The Self—Learned Helplessness—Spreading Activation
Stopping Stinkin' Thinkin' 12

The Wild Ride-The Dinosaur
Dump—The Limbic System 16

Cognitions—Internal Dialogue 19

The Bottleneck In Awareness 21

Information Processing:Top-Down—
Bottom-Up Processing Serial And Parallel Processing 24

Assimilation And Accommodation 24

Triggers Hard Wired And Hot Wired 27

Smart Brain Stuff
If Harpo Is Honking, Is Einstein Listening? 29

Warning Signs—Don'T Forget To Breathe 34
The Edge—Letting Go Of
The Anger-Vulnerability 37
Naive Psychology—
Looking For Your Clear Space Verification 39
Validation—Covering Your Six—
People As Social Beings 41
Finding Good Grief And Closure 44
Beyond Freedom And Dignity 46
Self-Soothing/Self-Destruction
The Pros And Cons Of Negative Reinforcement 49
Affective Tolerance Affective Repertoire 51
Learned Optimism 53
The Rip Van Winkle Effect 55
On The Beach The Pale Blue Dot
And The Existential Dilemma 57
Acceptance And Desire 60
The Pretrauma Self
Finding Harmony And Creating Synergy 62
Shattered Assumptions 64
Anniversary Dates 66
Watching, Reading, Hearing The News, Gives You The Blues
Tragedy And Trauma As Entertainment 68
Spitting It Out Or Swallowing It Whole 70
The Many Faces Of Anger 72
Dealing With Feelings And The Purpose
Of Psychotropic Medications 75
Wired Tired 80
Thoughts And Feelings
The Hazards And Emotional Miseducation
Of American Men 82

Deterrent Or Defense:
Using Assertive Communication Skills 85
It Takes A Long Time To Eat Humble Pie
From The Speed Of Light
To The Speed Of Mind 88
The Ten Thousand Meter Stare:
Doctor My Eyes 90
Cues Of Safety
Living Life In The Here And The Now
It's OK To Be OK 93
It's OK For Things To Be OK 95
Down In The Valley
And The Cumulative Effects Of Traumatic Exposure 97
Lessons Not Learned Are Repeated
And The Art Of Reframing 101
Boxes And Mirrors 103
The Problem Of Violence
From Frustration To Aggression 106
Flashbulb Memories And Flashbacks
From Feelings To Emotions 109
Slip Sliding Away:
The Nature Of Dissociative Processes 111
Anger Displacement
And The Anger Thermometer 113
Once A Warrior Always A Worrier,
Yet A Gentleman 115
Taking Stock Of Your Progress
And The Problem With Hope 117
Turn A Difficulty Into A Plan
Don't Turn A Difficulty Into A Problem 119
The Moral Animal 122
Rules Of Engagement 124

Sublimation And The Trouble
With Too Much Introspection *127*
Immature Psychological Defense Mechanisms *128*
Common (Neurotic) Methods Of Psychological Defense
For Combat PTSD *130*
Mature Psychological Defenses For Validation *132*
Hierarchy Of Needs For Combat PTSD *134*
Fixation *137*
Unfinished Business—Setting Bait For Trouble The High
And Low Road Coping Skills Bag Of Tricks *139*
Survivor Guilt
The Grieving Process And Finding Closure *141*
How We Sleep—Nightmares—Sleep Apnea—
Dream Innoculation Therapy—Sleep Induction Techniques *144*
Secondary Wounding, Indignation,
And Secondary PTSD *149*
Afterword *151*
References *153*

Foreword

◆

I am pleased to present this foreword on behalf of all combat veterans from the theaters of operation in World War I, to the Gulf War. Dr. Ashley B. Hart, Ph.D., had devoted many hours, days, months, and years examining the aspects of Post Traumatic Stress Disorder in combat veterans. He has given many veterans a hope they did not have prior to seeing him. He has on occasion taken that walk with the veteran. This book of essays is intended to help individuals who served in combat and experience problems in adjustment.

Regardless of conflict, approximately 15% of all combat veterans develop PTSD (Post Traumatic Stress Disorder). Mental health research has been able to identify several factors that contribute to the onset of PTSD, and in particular, combat PTSD, which includes the severity of the combat, and length of exposure. These factors are mitigated by age and level or responsibility. These are just some of the facts Dr. Hart will present in this book.

If you are a combat veteran, or a wife, or family member, hopefully these essays will explain aspects of combat PTSD to you. If you are a combat veteran and do experience problems in adjustment, I hope these essays are helpful to you.

Art Nottingham
Veterans Benefits Counselor
Arizona Department of Veterans Services
Sergeant Major, USMC, Ret.

Acknowledgements

————————◆————————

In putting together this *Operators Manual for Combat PTSD* I benefited from the help and collaboration from many peers and colleagues. I should thank first and foremost my operations manager, Eloise Rivera, who prepared the manuscript and endured numerous corrections and revisions in addition to her busy responsibilities elsewhere in my office. Kelly Turner assisted in formatting the manuscript for publishing. I wish to thank Sean Underhill and Ron Perkins for their assistance in developing the graphics and formatting the graphics respectively.

I want to thank Art Nottingham, Arizona Veteran's Service Commission, for his feedback on this work, and Harold Ruggles who provided editorial feedback helping this writer find his "voice." This was written for an ongoing PTSD group, and I would like to thank the feedback, assistance, and the opportunity to facilitate such a group for these veterans. We refer to ourselves as "The Thursday Night Gang," and over the years I have become more of a participant than a facilitator. In addition, I also wish to thank the collegial support received from the Veterans Administration Hospital Tucson, and their PTSD Clinic along with the Tucson Vet Center.

Ashley B. Hart II, Ph.D.

Introduction

◆

Recent publications report that the Veterans Administration currently is compensating over one hundred thousand combat veterans for post traumatic stress disorders while providing care, assistance, and counseling to another five hundred thousand. This manual has been prepared based on my past seven years experience working with combat veterans. These combat veterans have included Pacific, European, and African Theater World War II veterans, Korean War veterans, veterans of numerous conflicts and crisis including Lebanon in 1958 and 1982-84, the Cuban Missile Crisis, Dominican Republic, Panama in 1965 and 1990, the Vietnam War, Iran Hostage Crisis, Persian Gulf War, and Somalia.

I was trained as a psychologist, and psychologists are first trained as scientists before they learn the art of practice. As a scientist I was taught that there are lawful principles of behavior and that these lawful principles are ultimately based on an understanding of the laws of science. Psychology as a science is well within its second century. The separate scientific discipline of psychology was first identified as early as 1880. In my training it was pressed upon me that we are only beginning to discover the underlying principles and lawful nature of human behavior. The goals of this science of psychology include describing, or explaining human behavior, predicting human behavior, and controlling human behavior. This *Operators Manual for Combat PTSD* is developed with these goals in mind: To assist veterans with Combat PTSD in understanding the psychological, biological, and social principles of psychology in general, and Combat PTSD specifically so they will be able to gain self-control, and improve feelings of self worth and self esteem.

Within the past two decades, we have learned a great deal about how the brain works. A central tenet of current thinking is that people are the product of human evolution. This human evolution means that for people there are brain structures responsible for aggressive behavior. Usually, during our socialization process we are taught to refrain from using these aggressive brain structures. The problem for victims of Combat PTSD is that these primitive or aggressive structures produce chemical changes in how the brain works, and this influences behavior. Unfortunately, this change in how the brain functions leaves the combat veteran feeling extremely uncomfortable.

Seeking an understanding of the human mind and human behavior can be traced back throughout our own written history over the past ten thousand years. It is significant that the science of psychology, since the 1880s, has included this understanding of brain structures, and also interpretations of what now might be referred to as the software or the programming of the human mind.

When Sigmund Freud, a neurologist and the father of psychiatry, began studying human behavior, he developed a model of the mind based on an understanding through analogy of the human world at that time which included: hydraulics, an understanding of electricity, and comparative anatomy in exploring how squid axons or nerve cells behaved. From this, Sigmund Freud developed the first integrated or comprehensive model of human behavior (Id, our primitive urges, Ego, sense of self, and Superego, our morality).

In the early 1900s American and Russian psychologists began emphasizing the study of human behavior irrespective of what might be occurring within the mind itself. It was thought at that time that we could learn much about human behavior through what we can observe.

That is what we can see, what we can count, and what we can measure. These behaviorists, Pavlov, Watson, and Skinner, among others, believed that mental constructions of internal cognitive events were just speculation and not based on empirical observation. From this, an understanding of classical conditioning and operant conditioning was developed. This was referred to as the behavioral paradigm.

In the late 1970s and early 1980s a paradigmatic shift occurred primarily because of advances in understanding the anatomy of the brain, and, with this, the ability to begin exploring how specific aspects of the brain contributed to internal mental events. This led to the development of the cognitive and the cognitive behavioral paradigm. New findings in anthropology and carbon dating have provided a better understanding of our biological roots. This has led to the next conceptual scientific paradigm.

There is a current paradigm, which is integrating information from biology, psychology, and this is the evolutionary psychology paradigm. Recent advances in CAT scans and MRIs have given psychologists a better understanding of how the mind works and a consilience with other scientists who study behavior and how the brain works.

Consequently, the topics introduced in this manual were prepared after observation of veterans' reoccurring patterns or themes and from that information currently available within the science of psychology interpreted within an evolutionary paradigm.

Ultimately, there are two guiding axioms which are utilized to hold together this information:
1. The universe operates under a defined and definable set of principles which are unchanging and can be understood by man.
2. This natural and understandable organization of our physical universe, including the experience of life and the ability to appreciate our own existence, is this scientist's proof of God or higher power.

This leads to a postulate:
> Understanding the principles of human behavior, attempting to control Combat PTSD through this understanding, and a faith and belief in a higher power leads to an improvement in the quality of one's life.

Ashley B. Hart II, Ph.D., 1/6/2000

Keeping It In The Smart Brain Utilizing Spreading Activation: How To Use This Manual

Nothing is as practical as a good theory.

Kurt Lewin

There is, in modern science, a growing consilience among disciplines. Information from physiology, psychobiology, physics, chemistry, and psychology are helping us understand not only how the mind works from a molecular level, but also how the mind is altered through significant and traumatic events.

Recent research has shown that traumatic exposure can damage parts of the brain responsible for holding information in short term memory and increase lateralization or use of the right hemisphere which lacks language ability. Because of this specific damage, trauma victims frequently have trouble with short term memory, attention and concentration, mood, as well as sleep disorders. Because of this specific damage, other compensatory parts of the brain which are responsible more for anger and rage, even fear, begin to rule.

There is considerable research that shows that a specific part of the brain responsible for holding information in short term memory, the hippocampus, is damaged when individuals are in a prolonged stressful environment. Research has shown that the hippocampus can be reduced by as much as twenty percent in size. The hippocampus, more than holding information in short term memory, is responsible for projecting that information into the higher cortex or smart brain.

The hippocampus is believed to be largely responsible for the engram. This essentially is our working memory or short term memory. Typically, individuals are able to hold seven bits of information in short term memory plus or minus two bits (7+2). The fewer items able to be held in short term memory, the more likely a competing subcortical structure, the amygdala, is likely to determine stimuli are actual triggers for arousal.

When this occurs, the amygdala, responsible for rage and fear in a fight/flight scenario, leads ultimately to the production of adrenaline, and when this occurs the smart brain is overwhelmed by lower, more primitive psychological processes which are referred to in this manual as the dinosaur brain, and the adrenaline rush, as the wild ride.

What follows is a series of essays which were developed initially for an ongoing combat post traumatic stress disorder group. The purpose of these essays is to provide the veteran with a thinking man's understanding of combat PTSD. This is not an idiot's guide or a dummy's guide for handling PTSD. In order to allow the hippocampus to hold information in short term memory, improved cognitive structures need to be developed.

Cognitive psychologists have for the past thirty years provided information processing models of the mind. They have done so utilizing analogies similar to computer technology. With the advent of a better understanding of the underlying physiological processes there has been a growing confluence between these cognitive models of the mind and the physical structures which are actually handling and processing information.

Cognitive psychologists have shown through experimentation that we store information in our smart brain, our cortex, categorically. We store information by animal, vegetable, mineral categories, for example. When information arrives in our working memory, in this case our hippocampus, it is projected to our higher cortex where that information is sorted and sifted until the incoming stimuli is identified.

Through classical conditioning, certain sights, sounds, smells, become triggers for arousal. The hippocampus and the amygdala both process this information. If the amygdala has learned that these triggers are signs of danger, a fight/flight response ensues. The hippocampus, if unable to activate higher cognitive processes, then becomes overwhelmed. When this occurs, the amygdala rules.

As you read these essays, you will begin to form a pattern of understanding regarding combat PTSD. Over a period of time, through association, this pattern will grow stronger. This will allow your working memory, your hippocampus, to hold information in memory longer because of better top-down or prior knowledge about the world you are living in and the expectations that you hold for it. This prevents the amygdala from ruling.

The text of these essays have been highlighted. **The essential points will appear in bold type.** It is possible then for you to review rather quickly the essays by covering the bold print only. Doing this, when experiencing a low level of threat or anxiety, it is likely to help you achieve a sense of comfort and coping. **This is occurring because of spreading activation. The hippocampus is able to hold information in memory interacting with your top-down or ever growing knowledge base, and through the process of spreading activation allow you to extinguish triggers of arousal and assist in developing a more productive and satisfying life.**

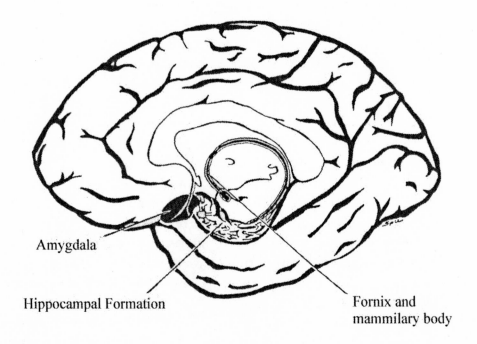

Amygdala

Hippocampal Formation

Fornix and
mammilary body

Location of the Amygdala and Hippocampal in the
dinosaur brain.

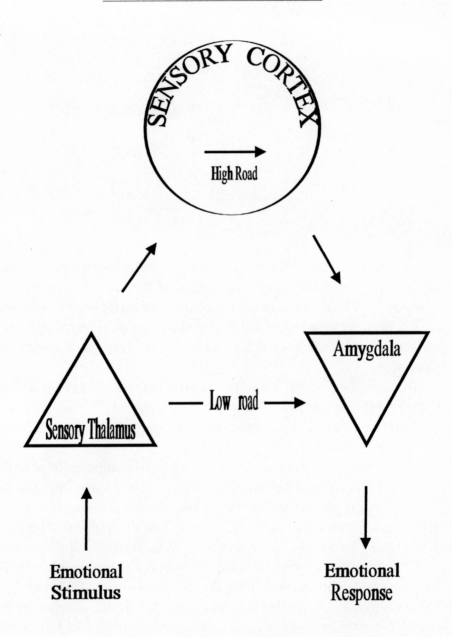

The Low and the High Roads to the Amygdala.

PTSD/It's A Stress Disorder/It's An Anxiety Disorder

A Post Traumatic Stress Disorder is defined by the American Psychiatric Association, in their *Diagnostic and Statistical Manual of Mental Health Disorders IV Edition,* as an anxiety disorder. You might wonder why an anxiety disorder is considered and labeled a stress disorder. In order to understand this it might be helpful to master the concept of stress and anxiety.

Stress refers to friction, a hindrance, a burden which interferes with a person's ability to carry out day-to-day functions.

Anxiety refers to the difference between what is happening in this moment and what will happen in the future.

A post traumatic stress disorder contains the components of both stress and anxiety, and caused by a traumatic event that happened in the past; that is post traumatic. Significantly stressful events have been able to impact an individual's ability to cope in the moment. This creates ongoing stress. The way this affects an individual and the reason why a post traumatic stress disorder is considered an anxiety disorder, is because of the chronic feeling of dread, apprehension, or hypervigilance. Combat PTSD victims have an expectation for the worst case scenario. It is not necessarily the moment that it is so troubling, but rather an expectation of what will happen in the future.

Awareness Of Thoughts, Feelings, And Bodily Sensations

One method of coping is an awareness exercise that provides circumspection of what is actually occurring in the moment. **This awareness exercise involves an examination of thoughts, feelings, and bodily sensations in the moment.** A moment is the briefest perception of time. Within each second, individuals usually are able to perceive between four to five moments.

When beginning an awareness exercise, it is helpful to take a deep breath let that breath out, in through the nose out thought the mouth, and to then become aware of what you see, hear, and smell.

What are you aware of now? What are you sensing? As you are reading this you may be aware of the words on the paper, the sounds in the room in which you are reading this, and the temperature, whether hot or cold. **You are aware of your thoughts or thinking, and you are also aware of your feelings** such as happy, sad, mad, glad, irritable, or angry? **We also have bodily sensations** such as the weight of our body against a chair, the weight of our body against the balls of our feet, any aches and pains, a sense of being thirsty.

Because post traumatic stress disorder provides an encumbrance of how an individual copes with the moment, use of awareness of thoughts, feelings, and bodily sensations can greatly reduce anxiety when coupled with additional coping skills such as breathing exercises, thought stopping techniques to avoid stinkin' thinkin', and visualization procedures.

The Nature And Course Of Trauma

Trauma: 1. Med. A bodily injury, wound, or shock. 2. Psychiatric.
A painful emotional experience or shock often producing
a lasting effect and, sometimes, a neurosis.

Webster's

Our word trauma has its origins from the Greek language *traumatose*. It is important for combat veterans to understand that trauma means wounding, and to be diagnosed with PTSD means that you have a mental wound. This is not a wound that is seen with the eye, but rather a wound that is felt by the victim. Because this wound is not seen by others, it can be ignored by society, and because it is a mental condition, a neurosis, it can be a stigma, but only if you allow it to be that. Our brain is the most complicated organ in our body, and when one is wounded because of horrific life experiences, this can affect the quality of one's life.

In order to be diagnosed with a post traumatic stress disorder, an individual must meet the criteria set forth in the DSM-IV.

The Diagnostic and Statistical Manual of Mental Disorders IV Edition defines post traumatic stress disorders through their criteria A through F.

Criterion A: The veteran has experienced, witnessed or confronted an event involving actual threat or death, injury or serious harm, and that serious harm involved intense fear, helplessness or horror.

Criterion B: The traumatic event persistently is re-experienced through intrusive recollections, distressing dreams, flashbacks, intense physiological and psychological distress.

Criterion C: Persistent avoidance of triggers associated with a traumatic experience and a general numbing or over responsiveness to these triggers.

Criterion D. Persistent and chronic arousal noted in difficulty falling asleep or sleeping through the night, irritability, outbursts and anger, difficulty concentrating, hypervigilance, and exaggerated startle response.

Criterion E: The disturbance is for greater than one month.

Criterion F: This condition causes significant impairment in social, occupation, or other areas of functioning.

Post traumatic stress disorders are described as acute, chronic or delayed onset. However, a growing number of mental researchers describe a post traumatic stress disorder complex with additional features. Acute post traumatic stress disorder is diagnosed if the duration of the symptoms is less than three months. Chronic PTSD is diagnosed if the symptoms have been present for three months or more. Delayed onset is diagnosed if the symptoms are at least six months after the stressor. Many combat veterans report some initial difficulty in adjustment, but develop severe problems later in life when there are other psychosocial complications which include increased responsibility at work, family dynamic issues such as divorce, separation, and challenging teenagers, for example.

A post traumatic stress disorder, complex, involves the above criteria but also includes dissociative experiences or fugue states and at times flashbacks so severe they render an individual unable to ascertain whether they are experiencing the world accurately or not.

Nearly seventy percent of combat veterans with combat PTSD also have other diagnosable mental health problems. The two most prominent are an affective disorder and substance abuse.

An affective disorder refers to a mood disorder, and of these the most common is depression. Depression in a clinical sense is primarily noted in a loss of interest in usual pleasurable activities. Learned helplessness and an expectation for harm contribute significantly to developing major depression or a depressive neurosis referred to as dysthymia. Typically, major mental health disorders begin in the midtwenties. Psychosocial stressors such as combat are believed to trigger these major mental health disorders in individuals who are both genetically and environmentally susceptible.

Substance abuse refers to the regular use of intoxicants with the expectation that that intoxicant will create a change in mood. Because this is a self-soothing but self-destructive method, many veterans have learned to rely on alcohol, marijuana, or pain killers to numb themselves to realities of the world.

How have you been able to share with significant others that you have been wounded although your wounds are not necessarily seen? When did you realize that you too have been traumatized by your wartime experiences? Most individuals who experience combat PTSD are also experiencing another mental health condition. The most common is depression, and second is substance abuse. If so affected, what have you done in order to cope with these conditions?

The Self—Learned Helplessness—
Spreading Activation
Stopping Stinkin' Thinkin'

*Life is all memory except for the one present moment
that goes by so quick you hardly catch it going.*

Tennessee Williams

We experience life in the here and now, and the here is happening in the now. This is what contemporary cognitive psychologists refer to as consciousness, and that occurs because of awareness in working memory.

What is that awareness? The first basic level of awareness is a sense of oneself.

The Self is the central character in a cast of characters, the experience, the one who is able to form and be conscious of an event. Brain researchers have been able to determine that there are specific parts of our brain that are responsible of this perception of oneself. Essentially, our sense of self resides primarily in our frontal lobes of our smart brain.

Those scientists who study how the brain works have found that **this sense of self rides on top of a series of more primitive brain structures.** These brain structures are responsible for sifting, filtering, and condensing information sharing only what is most essential with the frontal lobes of our cortex. Most of what our body is doing, sensing is not part of our conscious life. Who we are then, as people and as a person, is a conglomerate of these many cognitive operations that occur below a level of consciousness and to a great deal is predestined by our previous experience.

David O. Wilson in his text *Consilience* describes many of these cognitive processes. He reviews literature from a variety of sources as well as his own research concluding that people are the sum product of their own evolutionary history, past learning experiences, as well as current perception of the moment. **Primitive parts of the brain are responsible for initially sorting information, and we refer to this as the dinosaur brain.** It involves the amygdala, hippocampus, and other structures beneath the cortex or smart brain. **Everything that we see and hear is processed initially at this level before information is sorted and sifted and sent to the higher cortex. In doing so, similar events to the moment are identified through a process of Spreading Activation.**

Spreading Activation occurs when memory is triggered by current perceptions. These memories, in turn, trigger other memories leading to activation of cognitions which create ongoing internal dialogues. **Internal dialogues are those ongoing self statements or thoughts.**

Combat veterans sense of who they are as a person have been affected by combat experiences and experiences prior to combat. One's sense of morality, responsibility, and self-worth have been affected by combat experiences. As you look at yourself as a combat veteran, what conclusions do you have for yourself? Have you become your own worst critic? Have you developed a tendency to not view yourself in a favorable light? Have you created a cognition of yourself that is so unfavorable that whenever thoughts of your own existence come up a series of negative self statements ensue?

David O. Wilson, who was the first researcher to coin the phrase sociobiology observed that many inherited traits in people were

passed from generation to generation. He observed that people have a tendency to disrespect themselves and see themselves in an unfavorable light, and this makes it easier for us to work together in social groups. Being accepted and validated is necessary for one's self-esteem. A combat veteran may feel disenfranchised because of past experiences and how those past experiences are impinging upon working memory in the moment.

Feelings of Learned Helplessness can occur because an individual may feel that no matter which turn they may take, life can not get any better, that there are no longer any steps which may be taken which can improve or elevate one's situation. Siegelmann, who first observed the general adaptation syndrome where individuals under stress eventually break down noted that when animals were unable to escape from painful experiments that they would cower, curl up in a fetal position, and no longer try. He referred to this as Learned Helplessness. It is very common for individuals and combat veterans who are experiencing difficulty in obtaining validation and compensation to have strong feelings of Learned Helplessness. **This Learned Helplessness leads to very intense feelings of depression, and an ongoing pattern of Stinkin' Thinkin'.**

As previously discussed, **our own internal dialogues or self statements are predicated by our own biological hardware and our past experience.** When those past experiences are negative, and they are impinging on working memory, they can lead to this internal dialogue which puts down oneself or Stinkin' Thinkin'. Bad thoughts then generate bad feelings, and through Spreading Activation, create a series of even more intense dysfunctional statements.

As a combat veteran, are you aware of your own Stinkin' Thinkin'? Are you aware of your own natural tendency to disrespect yourself, to not feel that your personal efforts are worthwhile? If you have been able to transcend this experience, what tricks or techniques have you been able to utilize on your own in order to stop your own Stinkin' Thinkin'?

It is important to understand that hope is a feeling. It is an expectation of success tainted, however, with an understanding that failure is possible. But success only happens through effort. It takes once to quit, and those who are successful have learned to never, ever, ever give up. It is important to relable a failure or set back as a nuisance and an inconvenience rather than something that is truly awful, terrible, or horrible. By awfulizing an event or circumstance in the moment, you deprive yourself of an opportunity to find success and fulfillment now and in the next moments to come.

The Wild Ride-The Dinosaur Dump—The Limbic System

Psychologists who study the evolution of people understand that our brain has evolved. Our smart brain, our cerebral cortex, consists of three billion nerve cells, and the entire brain, the central nervous system, ten billion. This smart brain sits on top of more primitive structures including the mid brain or limbic system and the hind brain. The limbic system or the mid brain is responsible for much of the intense emotional responses that humans have. Recent research has indicated that structures within this limbic system, which are referred to as the dinosaur brain, include the amygdala, hippocampus, and thalamic relay. These structures work together to assist in interpreting information in our environment or triggers, and, if there is a conditioned relationship between these specific triggers a severe fear, fight or fight response can ensue.

As a combat veteran, you have learned that certain sights, sounds, and even smells are associated with danger. We refer to these conditioned observations as triggers. Everything that we see and hear is processed initially by this mid brain, limbic brain, or as we refer to it, the dinosaur brain. Information that we see and hear travels through our eyes and ears ultimately to the thalamic relay. These walnut sized structures, bilaterally situated beneath our cerebral cortex, sort information and send information to our auditory and visual processing areas in our temporal and occipital lobes respectively. This information is held in the brain with the assistance of the hippocampus which essentially makes an initial photocopy of what we see or hear.

If our brain, our smart brain, has learned and identified certain sights and sounds as potentially dangerous, this triggers the amygdala, two symmetrical structures, almond-like structures, even deeper within our dinosaur brain to begin making a series of chemical responses that ultimately leads to the production of adrenaline. When adrenaline is produced by the adrenal cortexes on our thyroid and on our kidneys, changes occur in our body. These changes involve increased respiration, blood pressure, and increased autonomic nervous activity. When adrenaline enters the cerebral cortex, or smart brain, this becomes a neurochemical transmitter which overrides the decision making and executive processes of our cerebral cortex, or smart brain.

When a significant event occurs and triggers the production of a full blown limbic arousal response, we refer to this as a dinosaur dump or a wild ride. It will typically take an individual three and a half to four days before this adrenaline is exhausted within the body. Until then, an individual will experience strong urges to fight or flee, and if this isn't possible, strong after-the-battle nervous shakes will occur. An individual feels their heart pounding and their body seems to shake within. This is a very uncomfortable period, and without management, this limbic response, this Wild Ride, will continue.

While we attempt to proactively limit and stop a dinosaur dump or wild ride, when this occurs, we have to remember that it is a fight, flight, or fear scenario. Use of deep breathing techniques and thought stopping techniques will slow down the process, but it still requires several days for the wild ride to end.

It is important to remember that planning is a method of fighting and dealing with the wild ride.

As a combat veteran you are aware that there are specific triggers in your environment which can lead to arousal. What steps have you utilized to identify these triggers? Use of breathing exercises and thought stopping techniques will reduce the probability that these triggers will evoke a limbic arousal response or dinosaur dump.

When a dinosaur dump occurs and you are experiencing a wild ride, what coping techniques have you utilized in order to minimize further harm to yourself and your loved ones? What steps have you taken to explain to those significant people around you that when you have such an arousal reaction you may need several days to calm down?

Cognitions—Internal Dialogue

At the top of the spinal cord and at the beginning of the hind brain is the generator which powers our body. This generator is the reticular activating system. It sends waves of electricity through our body four to five times per second. This flash of electricity running through our mind constitutes for us our perception of a moment. Our smallest individual perception of time.

This electricity operating at .17 millivolts travels into our brain where basic functions necessary to sustain life are automatically executed. During wakeful states there is an increased amount of electricity generated by the reticular activating system and this energy flows into our mind.

Over a period of time, having developed thoughts and beliefs, our cerebral cortex, our smart brain, has formed conclusions. This occurs when individual brain cells in our cerebral cortex, one of three billion, creates a chemical change that ultimately ends in the storage of knowledge. This happens because the DNA, the blue print of your body, produces RNA, and memory is stored through sixteen amino acids, coded and connected to other neurons holding memories and beliefs together.

As a consequence of this **we develop cognitions or beliefs. These beliefs lead to the development of an automatic internal dialogue.**

Mental health is possible but not probable. Human beings, people, are social animals. We gained dominion over this planet through our ability to work together collectively with other people. Because man cannot out run a cheetah, is not stronger than a bear, and can't out fight a lion, individually we would be quite powerless against other creatures on this planet. But working together we can collectively confront, and have confronted, all other creatures. **In order to work together in groups people have inherent within them concerns about how they are accepted by others, and also a sense which questions their own world unless accepted by their peers. This leads to a predisposition to develop dysfunctional cognitions which spurs on an automatic internal dialogue of stinkin' thinkin.'**

Combat veterans have a tendency to isolate themselves from others socially. Although we are social beings, combat veterans have learned that people are more threatening and more lethal than lions, tigers, or bears. Combat veterans also develop a series of internal cognitions regarding self-worth and interacting with others socially. There are hosts of other cognitions which are quite dysfunctional.

What are your dysfunctional cognitions? What problematic internal dialogues are you aware of? What pattern of stinkin' thinkin' have you noticed about yourself?

Over a period of time, by consciously confronting these dysfunctional automatic thoughts, it is possible to reduce the probability that this internal dialogue will continue. **Mental health is possible but not probable unless you take proactive steps to confront this ongoing internal dialogue.** Electricity will continue to pulse through your mind experienced as moments four to five times per second, and these internal cognitions that respond from an inner connected group of neurons will continue unabated without a conscious attempt to redirect them.

The Bottleneck In Awareness

Scientists who have studied the brain have learned that a part of the limbic cortex, the dinosaur brain which is responsible for much of our emotions, lies in the amygdala. This amygdala is responsible for emotions such as fight/flight, extreme fear, and rage. These brain scientists have also found that **this amygdala has more connections to the cortex, the smart brain, than the smart brain has to the neocortex, a more primitive part of the brain.** It might be surprising to know that emotions happen first before thought. Cognitive psychologists who study how we think, and more recently how we feel, note that under stress and tension our awareness, our circumspection, and our perspicacity of our environment is limited. **Under stress, a Bottleneck in concentration or focus occurs.** Consequently, we are unable to take in the big picture.

This has been well documented for individuals in combat as well as emergency service personnel and peace officers. When going through a debriefing of a critical event it is very common for the participants in a significantly stressful environment to remember only very selective and detailed information regarding their involvement in a critical incident. For an emergency service worker, for example, it is very common for a fire fighter or paramedic to only remember the specific steps taken in resuscitating a smoke inhalation victim. **In a combat setting, it is quite common for a veteran to only remember their own small detailed view of the war during a fire fight.**

Cognitive psychologists found that when a Bottleneck in awareness occurs, we are less able to remember significant events. It is postulated that this occurs because our working memory for short term memory skills, which is located in our hippocampus, can only hold a certain amount of information. Because we are focused on small and trivial details or the most essential details, less room is available for a broader and more comprehensive awareness of our environment in the moment. Interestingly, recent research has found that combat veteran's hippocampus or working memory, becomes smaller, while combat veteran's amygdala seem to grow larger in comparison. Because this amygdala is responsible for fight/flight has the ability to override the smart brain, the amygdala rules. Our higher cortex can only indirectly influence the limbic cortex. It does this by reducing the possibility that the limbic cortex, and more specifically the amygdala, becomes involved in our problem solving.

Psychologists have studied internal states for motivation. It is now possible to understand these internal states based on physiological models of the brain that have been developed by neuroscientists and cognitive psychologists who study feeling and thinking. One psychologist who historically has brought an understanding to internal states of motivation is Maslow. Maslow postulated a concept referred to as self actualization. But more importantly, for our purposes, is his understanding of the difference between deficiency needs and being needs.

Deficiency needs refer to man's basic needs for survival. At the lowest level is a need for food and shelter. This is followed by a need for safety and, this, by love and self-esteem. Maslow postulated that it was only when the basic Deficiency Needs were met were we able to become self actualized.

Maslow further postulated that only seven in one hundred people, at most, were able to live their lives in a state of being self actualized. But most of us can experience periods in our life when we have overcome and met Deficiency Needs, and rather are beginning to look for Being needs. **Being needs are evidenced by a need to know, a need to understand, a need to contemplate one's purpose in life.**

Only when we are free from threat and have a sense of safety can Being Needs ensue. As a combat veteran, what steps have you taken in order to seek safety, find nurturance, and develop love and respect around you including loving yourself? And, with this, how have you sought your own personal sense of validation?

It is only when Deficiency Needs have been satisfied, vulnerability contained, that it is possible to experience a sense of contentment. This is one's Clear Space. It helps to understand this concept of Being Needs to validate oneself while seeking tranquillity and develop a Clear Space.

Information Processing:
Top-Down—Bottom-Up Processing
Serial And Parallel Processing
Assimilation And Accommodation

Cognitive psychologists who have developed models on how the mind works have proposed that people utilize top-down, or prior knowledge which is stored in memory, to interact with the bottom-up data which is sensory input in order to make decisions and solve problems.

Top-down knowledge refers to prior experiences or learning. As a combat veteran top-down information includes certain expectations about one's environment and learning that certain situations, scenarios, or stimuli can be predictors of harm.

Data driven, or bottom-up information, is what we perceive through our eyes, ears, nose, and touch. This information enters our working memory. Neuropsychologists and other scientists who study the workings of the brain have identified specific cortical structures responsible for this working memory.

Data driven information is held in working memory by brain structures which, through electrical activation, communicate with stored information. This information appears to be stored categorically and by content or conceptual themes. Prior knowledge, or top-down information, begins generating hypothesis about what is entering the working memory through data driven or bottom-up intake. Once a hypothesis is confirmed, the self is able to make a decision regarding the information.

One problem with being a combat veteran is a tendency to misutilize top-down information and misperceive threat in our environment. Waking up with a sense of dread or apprehension is quite common. You might ask yourself as a combat veteran, how you misperceive your environment because of your past wartime experiences.

Cognitive psychologists also discuss two different types of information processing: Serial processing refers to step-by-step thinking, while parallel processing involves dealing with multiple levels of information. It is generally considered that our smart brain, our higher cortex, and sense of self usually is serially processing information in a step-by-step manner. Lower cognitive structures are processing multiple levels of information. It is only when this information is filtered down that step-by-step thinking is possible. At lower cognitive levels information is filtered and only that which is most essential is dealt with by the self's conscious mind.

A developmental psychologist, Piaget, described the process of learning involving assimilation and learning new information as accommodation. **In assimilation, new information is taken into memory and stored in preexisting categorical levels of organization. Accommodation refers to a process where new information is held in working memory, but does not fit nicely into any preexisting cognitive structure or top-down prior knowledge.** Because accommodation takes more mental energy, more parallel processing in order to incorporate new information and new learning, accommodation is much more difficult than assimilation. **Accommodation is frequently a source of frustration and a feeling of confusion.** As a combat veteran, information that is difficult to accommodate can be a trigger for a level of arousal.

As a veteran coping with post traumatic stress symptoms, what new knowledge have you incorporated into your daily understanding that has made your daily coping more efficient? How have you been able to stretch your understanding of yourself, your body, your mind, and your emotions in more accurately perceiving data driven or bottom up stimuli? What coping techniques have you been able to utilize to assist you in dealing with information that does not lend itself to assimilation into prior knowledge? How has a post traumatic stress disorder affected your perception of the environment? What steps have you utilized in order to challenge this dysfunctional perception of the environment?

Triggers
Hard Wired And Hot Wired

Psychologists and other scientists who study people have determined that we do have a few instincts and these include a suckling instinct, an instinct for grasping, but more than this, we **appear to be pre-wired or hard wired for a fight/flight response for certain specific stimuli.** As a group, people are afraid of spiders, snakes, and heights, and we also appear to be pre-wired to seek out or are stimulated by other triggers. This is usually best illustrated by an arousal response to secondary sex characteristics. Men are attracted to certain attributes of a woman's body and women are attracted to aspects of a man's body.

Based on our life experience we can become hot wired to certain triggers. As a combat veteran you are likely to have become hot wired to loud sounds, explosions, the smell of gun powder or oil, and that these sights and sounds can produce an arousal response.

These triggers are different from those that are hard wired or innate within us because they are learned. This learning is referred to as classical conditioning.

At the turn of the last century Pavlov, a Russian psychologist, found that if he presented a bell or a light before meat powder to dogs that over a period of time the conditioned stimuli (the bell or light) would evoke a response without the presentation of the meat powder.

This classical condition model is typically utilized to explain triggers that have been conditioned for combat veterans. Certain sights, sounds, preceded the presence of truly threatening events which lead to an arousal response.

Pavlov also found that if he continued to present certain conditioned stimuli or triggers without the meat powder or actual stimulus that over a period of time these triggers would no longer evoke an arousal reaction.

This is true also for combat veterans who have identified specific triggers in their environment which lead to arousal reaction. Because the trigger leads to an arousal reaction and defensive behavior such as avoidance, withdrawal, or angrily acting out, these conditioned stimuli or triggers will continue to be reinforced and evoke an arousal response.

The good news is that by identifying specific triggers and reminding yourself that they are just a nuisance and inconvenience, and by utilizing deep breathing and relaxation, and cognitively reframing these triggers over a period of time they too will extinguish.

What are your triggers? How can you learn to relable your triggers in a way that reduces the possibility that they will lead to an arousal reaction. What can you do to extinguish these uncomfortable triggers?

Smart Brain Stuff
If Harpo Is Honking, Is Einstein Listening?

Recent research has shown that our smart brain, our cerebral cortex which has two halves, a right and left hemisphere, demonstrates markedly different reactions for individuals who have a history of traumatic exposure. Trauma victims have an increased activation level in the right hemisphere. **The left hemisphere of our cerebral cortex is responsible for language and speech.** The left hemispheres is also responsible for body movement on the right side of the body, and reception of feelings, physical feelings on the right side of the body. **The right hemisphere is primarily nonverbal, or mute, and is primarily responsible for spatial relationships, music, and even is active in higher mathematical reasoning processes.** The right hemisphere controls the left side of our body. **The right brain is the source of flashbacks in trauma victims. Our smart brain has two halves: the left is Einstein and the right is Harpo Marx.**

In the early 1960s, Sperry, a neurosurgeon, treated individuals with severe epilepsy which began in the right hemisphere, spreading through the left hemisphere through connective neurological fibers through surgery in which he severed these neurological fibers, the anterior and posterior commissure, the superior collicus and most importantly the corpus callosum. This left the right and left hemispheres of the brain

29

function independently. He found through studies that individuals who were exposed to a ball, shielded from view, could not identify that ball by touching the ball with their left hand, but could verbalize "I think this has to do with fun or play, but I don't know what it is." In contrast, when the ball or other object was presented to the right hand, shielded from view by a barrier, subjects were able to easily identify that it was a ball.

There is even one reported case where an individual became angry at his spouse or friend and physically had to stop the left hand, which is controlled by the right hemisphere, from hurting the person by restraining the left hand with the right hand.

Recent research has shown that when individuals are traumatized there appears to be marked lateralization of activity in the right hemisphere. There also is a decrease in the activation or stimulation to a part of the brain in the left hemisphere responsible for language notably the broca area which is responsible for speech. There appeared to be a decrease in the amount of oxygen utilized by this part of the brain in the left hemisphere during the activation of a traumatic memory.

Cognitive psychologists along with neuropsychologists have known for some time that stimulation in the extreme left visual field is perceived by the right hemisphere and stimulation to the extreme right visual field is processed solely by the left hemisphere. These peripheral visual fields are not binocular and do not enjoy depth of field. The neurons that process this information are primarily transient rather than sustained pathways. We pick up movement in our peripheral visual field, and we orient to this movement by turning our head, able to see with both eyes, and both hemispheres of our brain, with our binocular vision or center visual field. Cognitive psychologists and those neuropsychologists studying brain lateralization have conducted numerous experiments to show this lateralization effect.

In the early 1990s Shapiro and her associates discovered a type of therapy referred to as eye movement desensitization (EMDR). In this therapy the person or client was asked to watch the therapist move their fingers across the client's visual field back and fourth. What this does is stimulate the lateralization response for the right and left visual fields. If this is done while thinking about a traumatic memory it has been shown to significantly reduce the level of anxiety that that memory invokes. It is thought that this technique allows the emotional response of these traumatic and pictorial memories to be reduced to just a flashbulb memory, a picture with an emotional response no longer, but rather just a feeling of sadness and a sense of loss.

One self-help skill that can be added to one's repertoire is based on the concept of survival, safety, and validation. By interlocking your hands, placing them behind your head so that one's elbows are in your respective right and left visual field, it is possible to begin an eye movement desensitization routine yourself. The first step is to make sure that you remember to breathe, taking three deep breaths and letting your breath out through your mouth and looking upward at something pleasant such as the sky, then with your eyes open bring your eyes down to a horizontal plain, recalling the specific trauma, and then without moving your head, just your eyes, look first to your left elbow saying to yourself **survival**, crossing horizontally across your visual field until you can see your right elbow saying **safety** then returning across your horizontal visual plain to your left elbow repeating survival, then to your right elbow, and doing this between five to ten times, inhaling and exhaling slowly and carefully until you again look up at a the sky or pleasant view stating to yourself, **validation**.

What this allows is for our left brain, which is Einstein, to understand what Harpo was so upset about. Many times the right brain senses danger. Its only method to communicate to the left hemisphere is through pictures, and those pictures can be interpreted as a sign of warning which you experience as a flashback or a strong sense of dread.

It is extremely important not to allow the dinosaur brain to become activated. By taking deep breaths and keeping your thought processing in your smart brain, it is then possible to utilize this eye movement desensitization routine. This way, if Harpo is honking, Einstein will be listening. Neurological pathways will be created connecting language and reducing this sense of dread which is being presented with painful emotional and pictorial images.

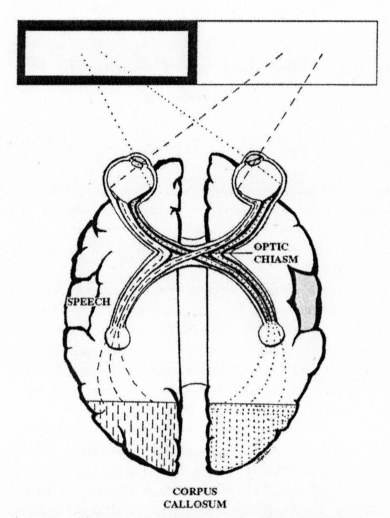

CORPUS
CALLOSUM

Lateralization: visual input from the right and left visual fields projects to the
cortex via connecting nerve pathways. The result is that the left half of the
visual field for each eye (right half of each retina) project together to the
right hemisphere of the brain, and vice versa. The corpus callosum
interconnects the two hemispheres to permit visual information
to be shared.

Warning Signs—Don'T Forget To Breathe

Conditioned Stimuli: As a combat veteran you, by now, are aware that certain sights, sounds, and even smells can be triggers for an arousal reaction. Many times we find ourselves mildly or, even more than that, deeply aroused before we truly understand what has triggered our arousal. Why is this?

We process information through eyes, ears, sense of smell, sense of touch, even taste, and much of this processing is done by more primitive parts of our brain. Our higher cortex, or smart brain, receives just the manageable amount of information regarding these sights, sounds, smells, tastes, and touches. Nevertheless, as a combatant you have learned that specific types of sounds, sights, or other **conditioned stimuli** are potentially dangerous, even life threatening.

Information comes in through our senses and is held in short term working memory by the hippocampus. Information is also sorted through another primitive structure, the amygdala, responsible for flight, fear, and extreme rage reactions. Certain events have become conditioned stimuli which the amygdala has learned as threatening. The amygdala will override the cortex and will begin an emergency response leading to the wild ride.

The wild ride occurs when through a series of endocrine changes the amygdala communicates with the adrenal cortexes located on our thyroid gland and also on our kidneys.

As a combat veteran you become aware that certain **conditioned stimuli** are likely to lead to an arousal reaction. If you find yourself feeling aroused, you can review the moments immediately proceeding your arousal or within the past day or so which might have been a trigger. While this is occurring, there is a chemical change in your body. Ultimately, it is the production of adrenaline which in our mind ends up primarily as norepinephrine. Norepinephrine is a neurochemical transmitter which leads to fight/flight scenarios involving the smart brain.

The Importance of Breathing: Psychologists who study the evolution of people have found that a common response to threat is that we don't breathe, and why is this? By not breathing, it allows the primitive part of the brain to begin the production of adrenaline which assists in fight/flight responses. Another **warning sign** for you might be noticing that your chest is tightening, your tongue is going to the top of your palate or the roof of your mouth, your fists are clenched, your biceps or triceps are flexed, and you don't breathe.

By not breathing, our frontal lobes, recognizing that there is not enough oxygen, communicate a sense of panic to lower parts of the brain, our dinosaur brain, and a chemical change occurs. **It is very important if you are beginning to feel aroused to ask yourself the question: Are you breathing? and if you aren't, don't forget to breathe!**

In beginning a breathing exercise, one of the best things that you can do is attempt to exhale first. Imagine yourself diving into a deep pool of water and working your way to the surface, and then exhaling quickly to clear your lungs. Then, through your nose inhale very slowly and deeply completely filling your lungs to their capacity almost to the point where you feel your lungs would burst, then exhale. The length of time that you exhale should be approximately twice as long as the time it took to inhale. You may count one thousand one, one thousand two, while inhaling through your nose, and count one thousand one,

one thousand two, one thousand three, one thousand four while you exhale through your mouth.

Visualization: As you do so you might want to imagine or visualize yourself being in a Clear Space. You might think of being on the beach or on the mountains, someplace that is calm for your to visualize. The sound of your own breath, inhaling or exhaling may remind you of the sound of ocean waves or wind rustling through pine trees. After you have done this three to not more than five times, you might do a half procedure of inhaling to the count of one thousand one and exhaling to the count of one thousand one, one thousand two.

When you have finished with this and the visualization it is helpful when you are experiencing intermittent anxiety to go ahead and take another deep breath or half breath and try for a moment to visualize this relaxation scene. As you notice yourself calming down give yourself a pat on the back for **remembering to breathe** and tell yourself that this arousal response won't last forever. If it is a minimal one it might have passed. If it is a major reaction you might be managing an arousal period that can last for up to three and one-half to four days.

As a combatant, your prior experiences have taught you that certain things are dangerous and life threatening. As you calm down identifying these **warning signs,** or **conditioned stimuli,** it is important for you to reframe that this was just that, and not something dangerous. This allows you to reframe what has occurred, and over a period of time reduce the probability that those triggers will lead to an arousal reaction.

The Edge—Letting Go Of
The Anger-Vulnerability

A complaint of many veterans with of combat PTSD is chronic anger.
This is in addition to those characteristics diagnostic of a post traumatic stress disorder which include intrusive memories, a marked startle reaction, and hypervigilance.

**Many combat veterans adopt a low level of anger and chronic bit-
terness which is referred to as the "Edge." This edge enables the veteran to maintain a sense of self control.** It allows the veteran to avoid
intense levels of anger and aggression. Typically, this edge is just below
the surface. A combat veteran may appear to others as friendly or
jovial, but those who know combat veteran well will describe the veteran as irritable.

In learning to cope with combat PTSD, a veteran frequently tries to
diminish the frequency of anger or angry outbursts and also reduce the
intensity of arousal responses. Maintaining a low of level of chronic
anger becomes an adaptive technique.

**It is possible to let go of the edge or this low level of chronic anger,
but it is necessary to pass through a period of vulnerability.**

Because anger is a feeling, letting go of this anger requires some cognitive restructuring skills. Relabeling triggers, becoming comfortable
and aware of your surroundings can be a precursor to letting go of the

edge or this low level of anger. Yet, a sense of vulnerability is likely to ensue. It is not possible to ignore this feeling of vulnerability for any great length of time before a more primitive part of the brain, the limbic system, or as we have discussed before, the dinosaur brain, leads to the production of adrenaline. When adrenaline is released from a full blown limbic arousal response, or a dinosaur dump, an individual is on a wild ride—a period of uncomfortable feelings and emotions for three and one-half to four days.

In order to avoid a limbic arousal response or dinosaur dump, a sense of vulnerability can only be experienced for a short period of time. This feeling of vulnerability can be tolerated at a progressive level of intensity and length. It is necessary, however, to use coping skills, breathing techniques, visualization exercises, and a sense of comfort in one's personal surroundings. With this, the feeling of vulnerability can be tolerated for a greater length of time and eventually the sense of vulnerability will pass.

It is only when these deficiency needs are met that it is possible to experience being needs and happiness can follow.

Depending on your progress and understanding of post traumatic stress disorder, have you learned to identify this low level of anger as the edge? Have you felt the vulnerability that ensues when you let go of this anger? What coping skills have you utilized in order to tolerate an increasingly longer period of vulnerability without an arousal reaction?

Naive Psychology—
Looking For Your Clear Space
Verification

Social psychologists have found that people develop a naive or common sense psychology about the internal motivation or states of others. As a rule, we look at other people and infer an internal mental state. We may look at other's actions or behaviors and judge them to be selfish, giving, caring, loving, hostile, caustic, cheap, or generous among a few internal states. Interestingly, however, when we look at our own actions, we as people, view ourselves as responding to cues or environmental stimuli. We don't see ourselves as having any internal mental states. Why is this?

The concept of cognitions and internal mental states is based on a collection of neurons which have learned to make certain judgments. We are biomechanical machines. As combat veterans, you have developed cognitions. Others around you are likely to see you as angry, hostile, bitter, and having a need to control. When confronted by our loved ones or others assertive enough to do so, we explain our actions based on specific events in our environment which are triggers which lead to an internal dialogue flowing from these cognitions.

As a combat veteran, what internal states have you been confronted with? Have you been described as someone who is not social, angry, bitter, short tempered, having a need to control others? Where does this come from?

A post traumatic stress disorder includes a history of past trauma, and the ongoing stress of the moment which is created by a feeling of dread or an expectation for harm. **Common among veterans, is to develop a very low level of anger or the edge in order to cope. Letting go of the edge leads to feelings of vulnerability.** The greater the sense of vulnerability the more likely this will lead to an automatic arousal response, a dinosaur dump.

In order to pass through a sense of vulnerability, it is necessary to have an understanding of what is on the other side. Balancing on the edge, feeling a sense of vulnerability, and letting that feeling pass, pay attention to what is going on in the moment. Be aware of one's thoughts, feelings, and bodily sensations. **It is possible to feel a sense of contentment in the moment. This sense of contentment is referred to as one's Clear Space.** Have you ever been in a Clear Space? Have you ever felt a sense of contentment?

One definition of love is this: Love is giving, sharing, and caring without wanting. The problem with wanting is, particularly if you are a combat veteran, that there is always a sense of dread, a sense of an expectation that things will go sour or things will go wrong. Understanding that we have this natural tendency to expect the worst and have this feeling of dread, it is necessary that we don't overreact to the moment, and that any conclusions you might have must be Verified. **Verifying and attempting to maintain a sense of the moment as a loving one by giving, sharing, and caring will help one find a Clear Space.**

Validation—Covering Your Six— People As Social Beings

Those psychologists who study the neuroanatomy of human beings and the history of people, conclude that we are social beings. For the past 100,000 years people, recognizable as such have become the dominant species on this planet. We have done so because of our ability to cooperate and work with each other. But this cooperation has a price.

Mental health is possible but not probable, primarily because of a series of preset, ingrained, and inherited tendencies to make dysfunctional self statements to ourselves regarding our own self-worth. People are inherently concerned about their acceptance by others and their acceptance by a group. This is biologically adaptive. People are able to survive because they can collectively work together and tame lions, tigers, and bears.

Studies on people have found that issues of self-esteem and personal self-worth are concerns to most of us. Psychologists measured the frequency of positive and negative self statements and the relationship of those positive self statements to feelings of self-worth and self-esteem. Using a time sample analysis, it was determined that people who felt good about themselves had a tendency to make at least fifteen hundred negative self statements to themselves each day. Examples of such negative self statements include: I am too tall; I am too short; I am too fat;

my skin is bad; I am not smart; I can't keep up; I'm not attractive to the opposite sex. Interestingly, this frequency of negative self statements was observed in individuals who had a good level of self-esteem and normal level of adjustment as judged by psychological tests. In contrast, individuals who felt poorly about themselves, and had measurable psychopathology such as depression or severe anxiety, on average made negative self statements to themselves in excess of five thousand times per day.

Why is this? Why is it biologically adaptive for people to make negative self statements to themselves? **By making such negative self statements it makes it easier for us to be part of a group, to be controlled by whatever people are telling us we should, ought, and must do. We only feel accepted and validated when the larger group sanctions us.**

As a consequence of being a combat veteran, we have learned that people are more dangerous than lions, tigers, and bears. We have learned there are certain triggers that may predict a life threatening situation. As a consequence, we are always on the edge. We need "our six" or our back completely covered, that there is no one behind us that we don't trust or there is a barrier which will protect us. Consequently, combat veterans have a need to have wall behind them or friends with them who can look over their shoulder to see what is behind.

This contributes to the anxiety or sense of psychological discomfort for combat veterans because we have a need, which is biologically inherent to be with other people, and have learned a strong distrust for the danger that people present. What do we do in order to deal with this? A typical response of many combat veterans is to isolate themselves and have a few places and friends where they will go and with whom they will confide in.

As social beings we need to be validated, and as a combat veteran validation often comes at the long end of the road of pursuing claims for compensation. **A sense of validation of one's self-worth and self-importance comes in part when the Veterans Administration, Social**

Security Disability, or Worker's Compensation acknowledges that you have been hurt or damaged by your honorable service. In the meantime, while claims are being processed, it is so common for combat veterans to become their own worst critic, to be unhappy with themselves and focused on their own shortcomings.

As a combat veteran, what steps have you taken to validate yourself, to improve your self-esteem and to stop your own negative self statements as your own worst critic? What other steps have you taken understanding that you do have social needs in your own search for nurturance? It is only when we let go of the edge and are able to manage that low level of anger that we can pass through a period of vulnerability and find a sense of contentment for ourselves and with those people with whom we share our lives.

Finding Good Grief And Closure

After war, **combat veterans experience grief.** This grief is not only of comrades lost, but also of a sense of self that has been changed by one's wartime experience. In war, the combatant is faced with death. In order to cope, combatants may conclude that they most likely may not survive and death becomes acceptable. For a very few is the halo effect and they are invulnerable. The most common reaction, however, is a sense of acceptance that death is all too likely. With this acceptance, a combatant is able to find a sense of self-acceptance. In that sense, the anxiety of war becomes more tolerable.

After combat or war, memories of those comrades, friends, buddies and sometimes one's enemy can haunt a veteran. **It is helpful to understand the grieving process, understanding how one may become fixated and stuck, and unable to find acceptance now after combat.**

The first stage is one of shock, disbelief, and denial. This can't be true.

The next stage is one of irritation. The irritation is focused. Blame is assigned. This anger can lead to combat veterans, long after their loss, continually tilting at windmills, searching for problems in an attempt to control, rectify a situation, and somehow undo past loss.

When this irritation or focused anger subsides there is typically a bargaining period in which we replay past events; such as significant anniversary dates of battle in which we can replay our own actions and the actions of others. In this bargaining we play a trick on ourselves keeping alive in our own mind our lost comrades and one's lost innocence.

As this loss becomes clearer, depression and a sense of learned helplessness is likely to ensue. There is a sense or feeling that one is destined to be doomed, even damned, not capable of enjoying the good life. From this, another more intense anger can develop, and many times combat veterans become fixated with this level of anger. This level of irritability can be extremely dysfunctional leading to a pattern of expecting failure.

The truth is that anger is perhaps the only emotion that a combat veteran truly is spontaneously capable of expressing until one has developed other coping skills. The good news is that if one is able to work through this anger, to draw it down to an edge, a low level of irritability, and to accept, on both a cognitive and an emotional level, loss, loss of friends, comrades, and one's innocence then it is possible to move into the final stage which is acceptance in which we accept emotionally and cognitively the reality of who we are, what we are, and what has occurred.

How have you as a combat veteran accepted grief as part of your own life experience? How have you learned to accept your own loss of innocence and loss of buddies and comrades, and been able to accept this and move on with your own life? If you have not, where might you be fixated or stuck in the grieving process? What can you do to avoid tilting at windmills or seeking a problem in order to vent one's anger, or lash out with cries of help and expressions of hopelessness? If this is so, how can you move through theses stages and ultimately find acceptance and closure?

Beyond Freedom And Dignity

Combat PTSD is initially acquired through classical conditioning.
Classical conditioning was first identified by Pavlov at the beginning of
the last century. He found that presenting a stimulus such as a light or a
bell before giving meat power to dogs led to a conditioned relationship
between those stimuli and what became a conditioned response. Pavlov
measured the automatic reaction of salivation.

With combat PTSD certain sights, sounds, and smells become triggers or conditioned stimuli for an arousal reaction.

**In the early 1940s psychologist B. F. Skinner developed a model of
learning and conditioning referred to as operant conditioning.**

**This differs from classical conditioning in that the person or animal
makes choices and those choices are either reinforced or not.** An individual receives certain stimuli and responds in a certain way, and, based
on the response, a relationship is either strengthened or weakened.

In the early 1970s B.F. Skinner wrote a popular book on operant conditioning, *Beyond Freedom and Dignity*. In this book written for the
general population, **he pointed out that we are conditioned by our
environment to behave in a certain manner, that certain reinforcers
exist, and much human unhappiness is the result of not correctly
understanding these reinforcers.**

His book *Beyond Freedom and Dignity*, however, was quite unsettling
to the general population. We like to be believe that we have free will

and a sense of personal choice and destiny. **Skinner pointed out that much of our actions are controlled through our environment, and that we have little choice in what we do and how we behave.**

Unlike other psychologists, Skinner and other learning theorists paid little attention to the internal mechanisms of the mind, referring to it as a black box. By paying attention to stimuli and reinforcers, SR relationships, these learning theorists were able to explain much of human behavior.

For a combat veteran operant conditioning is an important concept to understand. For the combat veteran operant conditioning and stimulus response relationships can have an important connotation. **What stimuli have you found evokes a set of behavioral responses in you?** Many times a combat veteran has learned to keep one's back to the wall, to maintain a sense of control over one's environment, for example, and, by doing so, are reinforced because this behavior prevents an uncomfortable level of arousal or discomfort.

Operant learning is also noted because individuals have learned, in a military environment, a certain level of structure and order is associated with a sense of control. Many times combat veterans find themselves uncomfortable when environments become ambiguous or less clear. This lack of organization is a stimulus, and can lead to a response of attempting to find order or fleeing in a need to find safety.

Learning theorists have also pointed out that learning is maintained and reinforced most when the reinforcement is variable rather than continual. That means that a number of responses are made before one receives reinforcement. Conditions in which reinforcement is predictable, and then reinforcement stops are more easily extinguished.

An example would be if one has been paid on a per day basis and the boss runs out of money and the individual works several days without pay. It is easier to expect that you will not get paid in the future and quit. A gambler putting quarters in a slot machine is reinforced on a variable-ratio basis, and one will continue to pull the slot machine handle for an extended period of time despite lack of reinforcement or reward through winning.

As a combat veteran aware that you respond to certain stimuli in your environment with predictable sets of behaviors, what have you done to explain this to your family? Understanding that variable reinforcement can make extinguishing responses more difficult, what can you do to identify those behaviors that require change so that you can lead a more productive life?

B.F. Skinner's point in *Beyond Freedom and Dignity* was simply that these reinforcers exist in our society. We still have a choice, but the real choice is to find those approaches to change which lead to reinforcement of productive and successful human interactions.

Self-Soothing/Self-Destruction
The Pros And Cons Of
Negative Reinforcement

The term negative reinforcement is often misconstrued as punishment. Punishment occurs in response to a behavior in which an individual receives a consequence such as a verbal reprimand, a swat or corporal punishment, or legal consequences such as jail and incarceration. Negative reinforcement is not punishment. Rather, negative reinforcement refers to the removal of a noxious, obnoxious, intrusive, unwanted condition or state.

Combat veterans frequently find themselves experiencing such a state which they find noxious, even toxic. Removal of that toxic state is reinforcing. That is why avoidance, bunkering down, even command and control can provide negative reinforcement by removing the veteran from that toxic environment.

Negative reinforcement can be self-soothing or self-destructive. When not taken to an extreme, those common methods of defense such as bunkering down, command and control, or on the road again can be self-soothing and not destructive to one's personal life. Taken to the extreme, it can be destructive. Self-soothing behaviors can also include those coping skills from one's bag of tricks which includes the art of reframing, stopping stinkin' thinkin', telling oneself that it is OK to be OK, and looking for cues of safety.

Combat veterans, as a group, have difficulty discriminating safety in their environment from harm. **Consciously looking for safety and maintaining a sense of learned optimism is a method of self-soothing.**

Self-destruction as a method of negative reinforcement can involve the abuse of intoxicants. Alcohol is a primary culprit in which an obnoxious or toxic mental state is dulled for the moment through intoxication. Other forms of intoxication can include abuse of prescription medications, primarily benzodiazapams or antianxiety medications. These can form patterns of behavior that are self-destructive when taken to the extreme. **Other self-destructive methods include thrill seeking, risk taking, self-mutilation, and even suicide.**

As you look at your own repertoire of behaviors to assist you in dealing with a toxic environment, **what skills are you aware of which are self-soothing and assist you in removing or reframing a toxic environment or mental state?** How do you explain this to your loved ones, your need to seek this? When you understand that you have control through using self-soothing rather than self-destructive methods of reducing and eliminating this state, you will feel a greater sense of self control, and it is only then that validation and happiness can follow.

Affective Tolerance Affective Repertoire

Life does not give itself to one who tries to keep
all its advantages at once. I have often thought morality may
perhaps consist solely in the courage of making a choice.

Leon Blum

Psychologists and other mental health experts who study trauma note that trauma victims have difficulty tolerating an affective or emotional state. These researchers note that individuals with PTSD, whether it be from mishap, natural disaster, combat, or a cruel act of one human being against another, have extreme difficulty with uncomfortable feelings. That is they lack Affective Tolerance, and they do not have an Affective Repertoire to deal with an uncomfortable emotional state.

Combat veterans, in particular, have a tendency either to withdraw or to exercise an aggressive, angry response to an uncomfortable event or situation. Have you ever been accused of being too gruff or withdrawn?

Day by day, hour by hour, minute by minute, and moment by moment, we make choices. The essential problem for a combat veteran is the tendency to make a moment, a life or death decision. In the give and take of our modern society researchers have shown that those who approach life in a tit-for-tat manner are more likely to be successful and enjoy healthy productive relations with others. Affective tolerance

51

begins with understanding this, and realizing that a win-win approach with others is usually the best and most productive solution to difficulties, decisions, or choices. In tit-for-tat relationships each individual gives a little in order to get a little. Over time, societies working in such a cooperative fashion have been shown to be more successful.

Developing affective tolerance or the ability to handle uncomfortable feelings requires the ability to listen to one's body, be aware of one's emotional state, and one's cognitive state. What skills do you have now in order to help your body to be more comfortable, be aware of emotional responses, and those skills necessary to reduce them to a feeling? What cognitive strategies do you have to avoid stinkin' thinkin'?

By realizing that life does not require you to take all in any one moment, it becomes easier to make choices and to tolerate life's discomforts, avoiding thereby the dangers of a wild ride or a dinosaur dump.

Learned Optimism

The difficulty many combat veterans face is the tendency wake up each morning feeling dread, apprehension, and an expectation for harm. This occurs commonly because combat veterans find it necessary to maintain an edge, and, with this expectation for things to turn out for the worst, they find themselves prepared.

Because of this expectation for harm, for bad events, many times minor events are misconstrued or seen in an intensely negative light. Have you ever been accused of making too much over something so little?

Because of this expectation for harm or dread, often combat veterans find it difficult to accept the world the way it is. There is a tendency to say things should, ought, or must be different from the way they really are. We compare our life to an idealized standard and, because of that, are likely to find it full of a host of plagues and difficulties.

One way of coping with this is to consciously look for the positive or the good in each day. This actively avoids stinkin' thinkin'. Waking up each morning and reminding yourself that you are going to have a good day, and that if difficulties come up you are going to leave them as difficulties and not turn a difficulty into a problem.

Learned optimism is an expectation that things are going to go right, and if they don't go right that you have the ability to be proactive and help manage or steward a situation until it is more benign if not correct.

It is important not to allow shoulds, oughts, or musts to interfere with your expectations. By accepting the world as it is, on its own terms, and then attempting to make one's life better, it is possible in a step-by-step manner to truly create a life worth living.

However, if we engage in negative self talk, **if we are our own worst critic, and we have an expectation for harm, we will surely find it.** It is easy to find shortcomings and problems in our environment. **With learned optimism, we develop an expectation for goodness and for things to occur right.** This can be a compelling force that will assist the veteran in maintaining a better sense of self-worth and will help avoid depression.

Too many times because of an expectation for harm, and an expectation that the world should, ought, or must be different than it truly is, a veteran will assume that they are not worthy of a life worth living, and, moreover, at times to somehow feel that they are damned or condemned to an unhappy existence.

To cope with this it is important to begin each day with a mental inventory of what you are thinking, feeling, and your own bodily sensations. It is common to wake up with a sense of dread, but that **dread should be relabeled as a cue to use coping techniques, a cue to remind you that, yes, you do have PTSD.** The thoughts that are stinkin' should be confronted by simply saying, I expect to have a good day. **I expect to enjoy my day today, and if something comes up I know I have the ability to cope and deal with whatever may occur.** It is helpful to review how one is feeling, physically feeling. Use of deep breathing exercises, relaxation techniques, and exercise can improve one's sense of comfort in one's own body.

What can you do and what have you done to achieve a sense of learned optimism?

The Rip Van Winkle Effect

So you are a survivor! Welcome Home! But when you came home from combat, you found that the world had changed. Just like Rip Van Winkle who slumbered for nearly twenty years, he found that the world went on without him.

No matter what conflict or war, combat veterans find that they have returned to a world, a country, a home town, a neighborhood, a family, that somehow has changed. Memories of home, memories of the world that sustained the veteran while in harm's way, that mental image sharp and clear has changed. Now that the veteran is home, that world that was envisioned, is a fairy tale just like the character Rip Van Winkle.

More than this, the experience of being a combatant has changed you. You are not the same person that you were before went to war. **Your experiences in the combat zone have changed you and set you apart, and now you feel disenfranchised from the home and the world you once knew.**

In previous editions of the *Diagnostic and Statistical Manual of Mental Health Disorders* one criteria of a post traumatic stress disorder included exposure to a significant psychosocial stressor such as war which most other people have not been exposed to. It was felt in those earlier editions, that experiencing trauma and having the experience uncommon for the general population was a necessary component of a post traumatic stress disorder. In the more current diagnostic manual of mental health disorders, the *DSM IV*, having a traumatic experience which others or few others have experienced is seen to be an aggravating factor. It makes the situation worse. **Because of this, this disenfranchisement, the veteran often feels set apart, alone, and isolated.** Although there is a need for some social interaction, that interaction is avoided by most veterans because of potential for interpersonal harm.

As you reflect on your own Rip Van Winkle Effect you may ask yourself how the world changed while you were away, how were you welcomed home, and how somehow you have been changed by your participation in combat?

What can you do now, understanding these components to overcome the effect of being disenfranchised?

On The Beach
The Pale Blue Dot
And The Existential Dilemma

Those scientists who study our universe—physicists, astronomers, and the like—tell us that we are a part of the Orion constellation. That is, our sun moves with the stars which we identify as the Orion constellation. We typically will see the Orion Constellation during the winter months shortly after sunset. The most striking aspect of the Orion Constellation is its belt, three bright stars in a line. With little effort it is possible to see those other characteristics which compose Orion— head, arms, and legs, for example. If we move far enough from our own solar system it would be possible to see how our sun would move and add to this collection of stars.

In the early 1970s a space craft, the Voyager One, left our solar system. As is did, it turned its cameras back toward our own planet and solar system, and in doing so took a picture of our earth and the other planets moving about our sun. Our earth appeared as a **pale blue dot**.

Carl Sagan, an astronomer, a physicist, and more than this, a scientist who was able to explain rather abstract concepts in a way which could be understood by common folks, wrote a book which he titled *The Pale*

Blue Dot. Carl Sagan pointed out in all our history everyone exists or has existed on this pale blue dot.

The other interesting thing about the Orion Constellation is the Orion Nebula which is near the center of Orion's belt. A nebula is a formation of hot swirling gases which form into stars. It is a star manufacturing center. The Orion Nebula within the Orion Constellation lies fifteen hundred light years from our earth. It is the closest star nursery, and many scientists believe that given that we move with the Orion Constellation that this is where our sun was born.

Our sun, according to scientists who study these things, is approximately four billion years old, and our solar system is also that age. Our star is a second generation star. Stars essentially consist of helium and hydrogen gases which are the simplest elements in the periodic table. All elements are composed of the same matter in that carbon which human beings primarily consist of occur only after a star has had a chance to live out its life cycle, collapse upon itself, and through the process of gravity, form more complicated elements.

Given this, it looks like our planet and our solar system are recycled star dust.

One of the greatest dilemmas facing any person is the end of their productive life as an adult. When a person is terminated because of a post traumatic stress disorder and unable to continue contributing, this is a very difficult time. We refer to this as **On the Beach. The truth is, sooner or later we are all on the beach. Sooner or later we are unable to contribute productively and whether we voluntarily choose to retire or others deem that we are not able to compete in the work force or contribute, it happens to us all.**

This is a very difficult adjustment and it leads to an existential dilemma of **what is my purpose in life?**

Ernest Becker, in his book, *Denial of Death* states that a common theme that all people have is attempting to transcend their own mortality through their efforts as a professional, as an artist, as a warrior, as a soldier, as a musician, or whatever avocation or vocation that is taken up. Those who reflect on their purpose and meaning in life typically look at their activities in a way that is deeper than what is first assumed. That is, one's position or accomplishments transcend one's life providing a meaning that can last longer than one's mortal existence.

When we end up on the beach and you didn't plan to be on the beach and you didn't have a chance to complete whatever task or activity, it is very common to feel lost. Even when you do plan to end one's professional or vocational activity, it is common to feel lost.

But the truth is **all of us on this planet, this pale blue dot, all six billion human beings that exist today are more than likely insignificant in the grand cosmic scheme of things.** But we do have the ability to appreciate where we are. We have the ability to appreciate art and literature, our own humanity, and in our ability to comprehend that there is something bigger than us all; that there appears to be a lawful nature to our universe. Through that, it is possible to find a sense of acceptance, that somehow as a mortal man with the folly of attempting to transcend one's mortality through our vocational efforts, then when we look at the big picture we can come to accept that there is something bigger than we as human beings, we as people. **If we find a trust and an acceptance that there is something bigger than us all, we can find peace with ourselves and find something to do which is productive while on this pale blue dot.**

Acceptance And Desire

Accept everything which happens, even if it seems disagreeable,
because it leads to this, to the health of the universe
and to the prosperity and felicity of Zeus.
For he would not have brought on any man
what he has brought, if it were not useful for the whole.

Marcus Aurelius

The roots of cognitive psychotherapy can be traced back two thousand years to stoic philosophers of the Roman Empire. These words by Marcus Aurelius can provide a helpful guide to combat veterans dealing with combat PTSD.

The first step in overcoming combat PTSD, is to learn to accept that one truly does have a post traumatic stress disorder.

Acceptance has two aspects: one is **cognitive,** and the second, much more difficult, is an **emotional** or feeling level of acceptance.

A combat veteran with combat PTSD may find it easier to accept on a thinking level that he has difficulty with a marked startle reaction, hypervigilance, intrusive memories, sleep difficulty, a tendency to isolate himself, but, yet, on an emotional level, have difficulty accepting this.

When there is **difficulty emotionally accepting PTSD, it is all too often expressed in the form of denial.** But it is helpful to attack this with a feeling. Unfortunately, most combat PTSD victims have difficulty expressing or even identifying feelings. Chronic anger, irritability is an integral component to PTSD.

In order to begin to heal from combat PTSD it is necessary to acknowledge on a cognitive level and a feeling level that one has PTSD and to confront emotionally and **accept PTSD with desire. This is a desire to get better.**

Many times veterans feel frustrated because they continue to be plagued with these primary difficulties and will express their frustration with anger directed at others or in an off-handed manner.

It is possible to reduce the anger to an edge, a low level of irritability which can be focused on specific steps or skills, coping techniques in order to feel better.

When one truly accepts cognitively and emotionally that they are a combat PTSD victim and that this is OK, it is then possible to begin to make true progress.

This is it. The world is the way it is and the combat veteran can begin to find harmony, a sense of balance, when **acceptance involves an understanding on a cognitive or thinking level and an acceptance on an emotional level.**

What can you do to channel your desire to get better in a positive framework? With true acceptance comes a sense of peace and validation and allows the veteran to begin living his life with a sense of meaning and purpose. Moreover, it allows the veteran to have an appreciation that they too deserve to have a life worth living.

The Pretrauma Self
Finding Harmony And Creating Synergy

Who were you as a child, an adolescent, even a young adult before entering the service? **Who were you before you were exposed to the trauma of war? This is the pretrauma self. It is a reservoir within you of rich, rewarding, emotional experiences in which you most likely felt loved, had a sense of happiness, and joy.**

It is possible to **draw upon this reservoir of memories of one's pretrauma self in order to develop a sense of harmony now.**

The notion of harmony is a helpful one and largely comes to us from Native American spiritualism or even Eastern spiritualism in which **harmony, a balance between oneself and nature, and with one's nature provides a sense of confluence,** moving together in a collected flow or harmony. We can find this balance with our thoughts, feelings, and bodily sensations.

If you are out of harmony now, you might take a look at yourself in your own current life, asking yourself, how am I out of balance? If I am out of balance, what specific change can I make to find a sense of confluence between my thoughts, feelings, and bodily sensations? Am I tensing up my body too much, giving me neckaches and headaches? Am I telling myself bad things? Am I misleading myself by saying the world should, ought, or must be different than the way it is rather than accepting the world the way it is and moving on? Do I find myself angry and out of sorts over little or trivial things? **Finding harmony with oneself is seeking that balance and making a small change in order to bring one into a sense of being centered or in a clear space.**

Synergy occurs when the investment of a little bit of energy leads to greater levels of energy. To make a correction you can use a little bit of energy to focus in on a deficiency, whether it be thoughts, feelings, bodily sensations, how you are interacting with others in small groups, social settings, how you are eating, what you are eating, whether you are smoking cigarettes or using another type of intoxicant. All of these can lead to discord, if carried to an excess. **Making a change, a small change, requires some energy, but making a change in an area that needs to be brought back into harmony will lead to a greater sense of happiness, self fulfillment and will release within you synergy.**

Synergy means that whatever energy you have put into yourself, circumstance, interpersonal relationship, you end up getting more— more than you put in!

Depending on your progress, you may need to reflect now on your own pretrauma self, your own times when you had a sense of balance and harmony, or now you may have the ability to more critically examine where you might be creating discord interfering with harmony. You might be at a level where you have made some changes and have felt the energy within you grow, or you have become synergistic.

What can you do to continue to make progress, finding confluence between thoughts, feelings, bodily sensations, deriving harmony, avoiding discord, and using your own energies to create synergy and a greater sense of self awareness, and acceptance?

Shattered Assumptions

How many a brief bombardment had its long-delayed after-effect in the minds of these survivors. Not then was their evil hour, but now; now in the sweating suffocation of nightmare, in paralysis of limbs, in the stammering of dislocated speech. In the name of civilization these soldiers had been martyred, and it remained for civilization to prove that their martyrdom wasn't a dirty swindle.

Siegfried Sassoon

Trauma victims experience the shattering of assumptions. This is true whether the traumatic experience occurred as the result of an act of nature, crime, violence, or being exposed to combat. Who were you before you were exposed to war? Your world was predictable, orderly, and you were spontaneous in your interactions with your world. **Once while in the combat zone your view of the world was changed irrevocably. Your assumptions were shattered.** From that day forth, the world was never the same. Can you recall where and when that happened, when all your assumptions about good and evil, hope and desire, want and need, were forever changed and tainted by your experience?

The way the world was supposed to be was bluntly changed. All powerful with your own weapons of war, yet all vulnerable as a soldier, a sailor, or airman, you had the ability to cause great harm, even death, to others and, also, by being where you where you were, in a position to be slain yourself. When you realized this you lost your own personal sense of being invulnerable and were overwhelmed with a sense of vulnerability. In that moment your basic cognitions regarding how the world worked and what you needed to do to survive, changed. **As a result of that you now carry with you cognitive distortions, even irrational beliefs of how the world should, ought, or must work.**

For most combat veterans with combat PTSD to avoid a feeling of vulnerability, you adopted an angry view of the world, a mean-spirited view of the world. You now grieve because of a loss of a sense of the world as being an orderly and predictable place, a loss of trust in humanity.

As a result of these cognitive distortions, there is also a loss of a positive sense of self-worth and self-image. The act of being a warrior was in fact a dirty, disgusting, and vial business quite different from the polished uniforms and hype of recruiting posters and vainglorious images of military life.

How has your understanding of the world been changed and shattered by your combat exposure? With this knowledge, what have you done to restore your sense of the world, putting those shattered pieces and images back together in one that is predictable, and, somehow in the process of peace, find a sense of order? What statements do you make to yourself in order to maintain a positive self-image, avoiding self-blame and avoiding self-criticism?

Anniversary Dates

Combat veterans usually have anniversary dates. These dates include the first time they were exposed to combat and significant memories of battles or fire fights. Many times these anniversary dates become triggers for an arousal reaction. Other dates, because they are important to us culturally such as the holidays, Thanksgiving, Christmas, New Years, Fourth of July, can become triggers for arousal.

Many times combat veterans report that they begin feeling ill, anxious, worried, have headaches, trouble sleeping, nightmares, as an anniversary date approaches and passes.

These anniversary dates are triggers which can lead to a level of arousal which can create a chemical change in the mind. This can create a wild ride where an individual is extremely uncomfortable for a period of up to three days as adrenaline is manufactured and enters the cortex as norepinephrine.

As a combat veteran you have learned to expect feeling uncomfortable during anniversary dates; even dread these. Many times combat veterans have a dread or apprehension for the holidays because of this level of arousal.

As you have learned to live with your anniversary dates and acquire coping skills, usually the impact of anniversary dates lessen as you come to terms with your own post traumatic stress disorder.

How have anniversary dates affected you, and what coping skills have you utilized in order to ease the impact? Understanding that anniversary dates are triggers like other triggers such as a loud noise, a bang, an explosion, the sound of a helicopter, or certain smells, how can you utilize your coping skills in order to reduce the impact of anniversary dates?

Are family and friends aware of your anniversary dates? What can you do to prepare yourself for anniversary dates and lesson the impact of your own emotional reaction on those around you and those whom you love?

One technique is to **identify thoughts of anniversary dates as simply a cue to begin utilizing your coping skills.** Breathing, stopping stinkin' thinkin,' monitoring your own progress through an anniversary date, and telling yourself that you are coping with this anniversary date better than you have in the past helps you reframe those dates so that eventually the intrusive memories which occur around and during anniversary dates can be reduced from an emotional level leading to a physiological change in your body to a memory framed with a sense of sadness, perhaps loss, and not a trigger for a full blown arousal response.

Watching, Reading, Hearing The News, Gives You The Blues
Tragedy And Trauma As Entertainment

One of the biggest sources of arousal or a trigger for combat veterans is a steady diet or exposure to news. Many veterans find themselves compelled to watch news twenty-four hours, seven days per week when they are not otherwise occupied. **This is one of the worst things you can do for your mental health.**

Psychologist's who have studied exposure to media violence since the 1960s have noted that such exposure leads to a heightened level of arousal, anger, and even acting out.

When you watch the news, hear the news, or read the news, you might pay attention rather than to the content of the news but to the advertisements. Typically, TV news contains advertisements for sports utility vehicles, denture creams, antacids, and pain relievers. Media creates stories, cover stories, and emphasize the stories which garner the highest number of viewers.

Despite the fact that within the past ten years the number of youngsters killed by handguns at school, people injured in violent crimes, people killed in automobile accidents or aircraft disasters have been significantly reduced or lessened, many people's perception is that more children are being killed at school, or people are being raped or murdered, and more people are being injured in violent car accidents, and aircraft accidents. Why is this? With the advent of cable and satellite TV more stations are available for the news, and people seem to like a diet of this. People enjoy watching trauma and tragedy as entertainment. Rather than rubber necking or looking back at a highway accident we can, through mini-cams and satellite transmissions, watch trauma unfolding before our very eyes.

What does this do for the veteran? **It is a trigger for arousal.** It leads to the production of adrenaline and dysfunctional self statements or stinkin thinkin and wearisome worrying, and over the long run, because you can not do anything about what you are observing on TV news, you are going to feel helpless and you will feel the blues.

The best advice for combat veterans is to limit one's exposure to the news, and if you feel a compelling need to follow a particular story do so with the printed page. **Remember, hearing, reading, or watching the news will give you the blues.**

Spitting It Out Or Swallowing It Whole

In this world a man must either be a hammer or an anvil.

Henry Wadsworth Longfellow

As a combat veteran you surely are better off if you can prevent yourself from becoming angry and, if you are angry, to reduce it to its lowest level, the edge. However, if you can't shake the anger, the trick is to keep it from becoming an emotion; just a feeling. An emotion involves a change in the physiological functioning of the body while a feeling does not.

What do you do with your anger? Does your wife and do loved ones complain because you take out your anger on them, or do you keep it within?

When we are angry we have two choices: to either spit it out or swallow it whole. Either way, using one approach to deal with your anger exclusively will create long-term and harmful consequences.

If you spit your anger out on others you will drive them away and you will find yourself without love and nurturance. Have you ever found yourself being rejected by those you love the most?

If you swallow your anger whole, you will become sick. You can become so afraid that you will lack energy, be reluctant to leave your home, your room, or you might find yourself feeling tremendously depressed and sad.

People who swallow their anger all the time can develop major medical problems. Individuals who are unable to express hostility and lack self-assertion frequently are cancer victims in comparison to others. This has been referred to as a cancer profile.

Continually being aroused and angry is often associated with heart disease and hypertension. Continually spitting out your anger on others can have a significant impact on your cardiovascular health.

As Longfellow advises: "In this world a man must either be a hammer or an anvil." Using feelings of anger constructively, it is possible for the veteran to sublimate his energy into creative activities. Many times combat veterans who feel angry will busy themselves in a project, or might find themselves straightening or restraightening a room with files or their possessions.

As an anvil, a veteran might find himself stubbornly insisting on a course of action, unbending, and this steadfastness can be a source of support for others in times of trouble.

How do you handle anger? What steps do you utilize to minimize your anger? **If you are unable to reduce your anger to its lowest level, it is important not to rely on spitting it out or swallowing it whole exclusively,** but find ways to vent, minimize, and channel this feeling into actions which are productive rather than destructive.

The Many Faces Of Anger

God, grant me the serenity to accept the things I cannot change,
Courage to change the things I can,
and The wisdom to know the difference.

A.A. Serenity Prayer

Anger is a term which refers to a host of feelings, and anger, chronic anger, is a central component to combat post traumatic stress disorders. **Anger is defined broadly in feelings of resentfulness, revenge, and displeasure.** Others may interpret anger as including feeling mad, irritated, ticked, but anger also implies a source. For many combat veterans the source of anger is confused by significant others in their life. Many times the combat veteran's spouse or significant other may misinterpret a veteran's feeling as if they are angry with themselves or others.

There are many faces or sources of anger, and the source of anger may be within yourself, with a situation, or with others.

It is important for the combat veteran to understand the source of anger, and to attempt to keep anger a feeling rather than an emotion. It is first helpful to identify the source, whether it be with oneself, situation, or with others. Further, it is helpful to clarify the source with loved ones so that one's anger is not assumed to be directed at them, when it is not.

A combat veteran may find himself angry with himself, and within himself he can be angry at his actions, past actions, thoughts, feelings, or angry at one's pain—physical pain, mental pain, or anguish.

We can find ourselves angry at a situation. One problem that occurs is when we believe the world should, ought, or must be different than the way it is. The truth is that the world is the way it is. By accepting the world on its own terms, it makes it easier to develop a plan and cope. Shoulds, oughts, or musts, when used to define the world or situation the way it is, obscure the facts. The essence of the AA Serenity Prayer is accepting life on its own terms, accepting that which we can change, that which we can't, and having the wisdom to understand the difference among these.

Anger at others can occur, does occur, and will occur. It is helpful when we discover our anger at others to focus on how we arrived at such a feeling. Is our anger justified? Are we evaluating others' behaviors from our own perspective? Or are we angry at others because they are ignorant? Are we angry at others because they fail to fulfill our expectations of what they should have done, ought to have done, or could have done?

On the other side of the spectrum from anger and hate is grief and loss. We can find ourselves angry with ourselves for not feeling grief, angry with ourselves for not being able to feel loss, angry with ourselves because we can't find pleasure, and that forbearance, tolerance, and patience are difficult virtues to hone.

There are many faces of anger, and anger is best kept in check by catching dysfunctional thoughts and not allowing anger to grow, and remembering that pleasure, tolerance, and forbearance are antidotes to anger.

What can you do and what have you done to limit your anger, to identify the nature of these uncomfortable feelings, and to assist others in feeling as comfortable around you as you would like to feel yourself?

What have you done to let your loved ones know that your anger is not with them, but a sense of discomfort and uneasy tension that arises from a continual need to ever remain vigilant?

Dealing With Feelings And The Purpose Of Psychotropic Medications

The reason we have feelings—happy, sad, mad, glad, angry, terrified, in love, or hate—is to alert ourselves to an occurrence, a significance, or the nature of some subjective experience. The self many times becomes aware of the importance of a circumstance through emotions. Many combat veterans have learned that emotions are uncomfortable, and have learned to deal with emotions by tuning out or numbing them out. Emotions for combat veterans can be painful. Two common states are anxiety and anger. Anxiety can be characterized by an intense feeling of dread. Anger is a strong sense of resentment about a situation, person, or personal circumstance.

Recent literature has shown that learning to identify feelings through verbalizing somatic states or how one's body feels may be an important way to learn about feelings themselves. Heart palpitations, upset stomach, tight muscles, headaches, and neck cramps are many times signs of these emotional states. In the 1880s and '90s physicians described Civil War veterans with "battle heart," a condition in which Civil War veterans were waking early in the morning with a strong thumping heart. These veterans were quite concerned that this would effect their mortality, but on closer examination these veterans were experiencing the complications of ongoing life rather than a life threatening heart condition.

Medications are important to help manage emotional states initially following traumatic exposure. The purpose of these medications primarily is to assist veterans in reducing anxiety, alleviating depression, and improving concentration skills by reducing the possibility of psychological numbing.

Medication for combat PTSD is utilized because of changes in the biological functioning of the individual exposed to trauma. There are four primary reasons for medication intervention:

The first is the dinosaur dump or rather noradrenergic disregulation, sometimes referred to as norepenephrine, adrenaline has been converted by the body into a neurochemical transmitter. It leaves the smart brain and more primitive parts of the brain in a fight/flight or fear mode.

Second, our body can only make serotonin if we are in a wakeful, restful, state. Serotonin activity is disrupted by the presence of the increased amount of an adrenaline related neurochemical, or norepenephrine. Because of serotonin problems, we end up with difficulty sleeping, increased irritability, and impulse problems.

Third, referred to as "kindling," is the lowering a threshold response for additional dinosaur dumps or wild rides. The intrusive symptoms act as a trigger for further emotional response creating physiological changes in neurochemical levels and functioning.

Fourth, combat veterans have an increased startle response. In fact, studies have shown that combat veterans never habituate to sharp, loud, or sudden sounds. Startle responses remain a persistent symptom of PTSD even after lengthy therapeutic intervention.

Different medications have very specific purposes of intervention. The first group, antianxiety medications or benzodiazapams, may be helpful initially in dealing with acute trauma, but are only necessary for individuals who experience ongoing marked startle responsiveness

with increasingly intrusive thought, arousal and anxiety reactions. Benzodiazapams appear to reduce anxiety and block the limbic system from overreacting to intrusive symptoms. The down side to these minor tranquilizers is that they are addicting and withdrawal from benzodiazapam is a very uncomfortable process that precipitates increased startle responses and emotional reactions.

The second group includes the serotonin re-uptake inhibitors. These include medications such prozac, zoloft, luvox, and paxil. This medication is very effective in the long run in suppressing the kindling effect because it increases the amount of serotonin available and will have a calming effect. This medication inhibits the amygdala from overriding other more primitive brain structures. This is not an addicting medication, but its down side is that it will interfere, at times, with sexual functioning and sexual arousal. What appears to occur with combat veterans who are utilizing SSRIs is that their attention and concentration improves and they are less bothered by intrusive thoughts or psychological numbing. These medications take up to three to four weeks to begin having an effect.

A third medication intervention are trycyclic antidepressants. This is an older group which has a shotgun effect on catecholomines or neurochemical transmitters and include medications such as amatriptaline, imipramine, desipramine, and trazodone. These medications seem to work best with individuals who have a lower level of combat exposure, but are bothered by feelings of guilt, somatic anxiety, and impaired concentration. These medications have been shown to improve sleep patterns. Typically, these medications take up to four to five weeks before the effects are felt.

Another group of medications have been referred to in the psychiatric literature as mood stabilizers, but they are truly anticonvulsants. These include medications such as carbamazepine, and valproic acid. These medications appear to be helpful with chronic PTSD, particularly those involving dissociative features. It is less likely for our brain's neurons to fire on their own when taking these anticonvulsants.

Another group includes the alpha 2-adrendrgic agonists and the beta-adrendrgic blockers. Clonidine is an example an alpha adrendrgic agonist. It has been found to be helpful with individuals who have a tendency to self-mutilate themselves and also abuse intoxicants. Propranolol, a beta adrenergic blocker, has been seen to be helpful with individuals who demonstrate explosiveness, severe nightmares, and severe intrusive recollections along with sleep impairment. This medication has been shown to improve self-esteem and psychosocial functioning. The down side with these include poor memory, feelings of depression, and tiredness.

Atypical antidepressants include bupropion, (wellbutrin), and venlafaxine (effexor). These medications help with treatment resistant patients who have not benefited from SSRIs or tricyclics. These medications have improved serotonergic and dompaminergic levels.

Newer medications are being developed which will have both SSRI and tryclic properties. Effectiveness with combat PTSD has not been demonstrate in clinical trials. Effexor (venlafaxine) is thought to have both of these properties.

Psychologists see medications as another tool. When behavioral interventions are not effective in and of themselves medications may be suggested by psychologists and social workers working with individuals experiencing combat PTSD. Psychiatrists and behavioral neurologists are specialists with these medications.

There are homeopathic medications available or herbal medications that can be used as well. Valerian root has been used for over two thousand years to assist with feelings of anxiety, marked startle reaction, and to improve sleep.

St. John's Wort assists in improving serotonin levels, but to be effective for an adult man of average weight 900 mgs. needs to be taken. This medication or herbal should be taken early in the morning.

Melotonin is another herbal, which improves serotonin levels and can improve sleep patterns. This also has been reported to assist an individual in maintaining a sense of calm, tranquility and a restful, wakeful state.

Aside from the benzodiazapams, most of these medications do not have immediate effects with PTSD symptoms other than initial drowsiness with the tricyclic medications and the benzodiazapams. Rather, after several weeks an individual will find themselves feeling better taken by surprise with a feeling of tranquility and experiencing a clear space.

Wired Tired

Rule Number One: Life is a struggle.
Scott Peck

Many combat veterans report feeling **wired tired**, unable to relax, feeling exhausted, yet unable to fall asleep at the end of a day. Many veterans live a life characterized by a quiet tension which leaves them feeling drained and exhausted, yet wired. Why is this?

Our brain manufactures its own neurochemicals. There is one group of neurochemicals that are manufactured during the day, and another group of neurochemicals that are manufactured while we sleep. The neurochemical made by our brain when we are in a peaceful, restful, wakeful state primarily is serotonin. Serotonin, when it builds to a sufficient level in the body, allows an individual to fall asleep.

If during the day, however, you have had an arousal response, a bit of a wild ride, you might find yourself at the end of the day feeling edgy, exhausted, tired, and wired.

You may lay in bed and toss and turn bothering your spouse or partner only to get up and occupy yourself until you eventually feel exhausted. Many times up in the wee hours of the night when the world is quiet, a veteran can find those solitary activities that lead to being in a peaceful, restful state. **Serotonin builds and the biological clock that allows for sleepy feelings and slumber eventually ensues.**

While we are asleep in a restful, not agitated slumber, our body manufactures another group of neurochemicals. These neurochemicals include dopamine and acetylcholine. If we have disruptive or fitful sleep, then our body is not able to manufacture enough of these neurochemicals and we will wake in the morning feeling edgy, full of dread.

Certain medications attempt to compensate for serotonin while others provide a shotgun approach attempting to provide replacements for all major neurochemicals. While many neurochemical transmitters have been identified, the primary ones remain serotonin, dopamine, and acetylcholine. The more recent antidepressants are serotonin re-uptake inhibitors, the SSRIs, include drugs such as paxil, prozac, and zoloft (paraxetine, fluoxetine, sertraline respectively) while other older drugs, the tricyclics, include medications such as elavil, desyrel, sinequan, and tofranil (amitriptyline, trazodone, doxepin, and imipramine, respectively).

Do you frequently find yourself feeling wired tired? What can you do about this? The best advise is to remember to manage the moment. Don't forget to breathe, understanding that serotonin is naturally built up in your body when you are in wakeful, restful state. Try to occupy yourself by piddling. Sublimate your activities so that your mind does not wander into stinkin' thinkin' which can lead to agitation.

Preparation for sleep can also include deep breathing and reminding yourself that if you have a nightmare, that you can sleep through the night or at least recognize that you are in a bad dream with the potential to change and rearrange that dream.

Being wired tired is just another complication from combat PTSD, but understanding what it is leads to natural coping strategies. What coping strategies have you found are helpful? How can you continue to apply these in your daily life so that at the end of the day you are not wired, just tired?

Thoughts And Feelings
The Hazards And Emotional
Miseducation Of American Men

Developmental psychologists who study emotional processes in infants through adulthood note that initially as infants, human beings have four distinct emotional states: pleasure, displeasure, pain, and satisfaction. From these basic emotional states more complicated feelings eventually emerge.

Scientists who study the development of the human brain have determined that we initially experience feelings or emotions such as happy, sad, mad, and glad, and that **these emotional and feeling states begin at a subcortical or dinosaur brain level.** These feelings and emotional states are **later transcribed into thoughts by higher cortical processes.**

Unchecked, uncomfortable feelings lead to stinkin' thinkin' and stinkin' thinkin' leads to uncomfortable emotional responses such as anger and rage. **For many combat veterans only anger as a feeling or an emotion is easily expressed.**

These scientists who study brain and human emotional development have determined that we experience emotions and feelings first, and this begins as a more primitive response which is later processed into thoughts. What is a thought? A thought is characterized by thinking, reflection, conceiving ideas, cause and effect relationships, this results in that, and so forth.

Contemporary psychologists have noted that the way American boys and men have been educated regarding their feelings and emotions has created a functional hazard in how males approach life. In a popular self-help book published in the mid '70s, the *Hazards of Being Male,* the author pointed out that most men have been reared in an environment which allowed few, if any, direct emotional expressions. These included: happy, sad, mad, glad, and, occasionally, under the correct circumstances, indignation or rather righteous anger. Recent psychological publications report that emotional miseducation of men in our society continues. Most feelings are not allowed.

As you reflect on your own pretraumatic history, what emotional reactions were appropriate in your home, your neighborhood, and in your community?

During training and as a combatant, what emotional responses and feeling responses were considered appropriate?

The truth is, that most of us have difficulty differentiating between thoughts and feelings. Feelings, such as happy, sad, mad, glad, simply exist. They are like a cloud in the sky. It might be puffy and white, gray and threatening; but, it simply is. A thought usually contains a cause and effect relationship, an intuition, a conclusion.

Many times we have difficulty integrating our own thoughts and feelings, so that there is not a confluence between thoughts and feelings. We may strive for a sense of contentment which is a feeling through positive thinking, deliberately avoiding stinkin' thinkin', but yet still feel a sense of dread or apprehension.

It takes time to find a confluence between thoughts and feelings. When thoughts are positive and feelings are positive, and one senses that one's body is relaxed, it is possible to have a sense of spontaneity in life and experience the emotion of fun.

When was the last time you had fun and laughed, and felt a sense of spontaneity between your thoughts and feelings, and a happiness within your body?

For many combat veterans, finding that true confluence begins with a search for one's own personal history and pretraumatic self. Exploring happiness in childhood is one method to again find a clear space and enjoy a sense of contentment and fulfillment in the moment.

Deterrent Or Defense: Using Assertive Communication Skills

Keep strong, if possible. In any case, keep cool.
Have unlimited patience. Never corner an opponent,
and always assist him to save face.
Put yourself in his shoes—so that you see things through his eyes.
Avoid self righteousness like the devil—nothing so self-blinding.

Basil Hart

Combat veterans are trained for war, but not trained for peace aside from their own pretrauma history. Because of this, there is a natural tendency to push the limit with those we interact with and to become too aggressive. In order to avoid feelings of vulnerability combat veterans adopt an edge, a low level of anger. While this provides a level of security, it can have detrimental effects on maintaining and sustaining successful relationships with others, and can be a precursor for acting out with consequences affecting the veteran interpersonally, occupationally, even legally.

The trick is to learn to express yourself without becoming hostile. One method to do this is referred to as assertive communication. In order to understand what assertive communication is, it is helpful to understand what it is not. Assertive communication is not hostile.

Hostile actions are normally described as anger directed specifically at a person. Hostile actions can take the form of blaming and complaining about those around you or others whom you find to be significantly impeding your goals.

Assertive communication is neither passive nor nonassertive communication. Nonassertive or passive communication occurs when we ask others to evaluate us, or when we ask others to evaluate their own choices such as why do you do this, or why do you do that? The difference from hostile communication is that hostile communication involves verbally and belligerently putting someone down or at the same time blaming, complaining, or evaluating their behavior.

In either case, **both hostile and nonassertive communication prevent you from communicating with significant others in an adult-to-adult manner.** In hostile communication you are top downing by evaluating significant others around you and placing them in a subservient or child-like position. In order to continue the communication with you the recipient must assume a child-like role or break the communication pattern. In a nonassertive or passive communication style you become the child asking someone else to evaluate your behavior and what should, ought, or must happen.

The central and key method of maintaining adult-to-adult assertive communication is to use the I Message. An example of an I message would be, I feel frustrated when I am not allowed to have my own uninterrupted personal space. Sometimes I feel angry, and when I feel angry, I like to go outside or take a walk. I am not angry with you. I just feel angry and need to chill out. This is much more effective than blaming someone for your own frustrations.

When using assertive communication with significant others, being able to understand your spouse, or significant other's point of view is essential. I understand that you think, I understand that you feel…and this can be followed by and I feel this about that.

The essential point is to describe a behavior and a feeling using an I message. For example, I feel _____ when_____. Such as, I feel upset when my things are disturbed. This allows your significant others to respond in a more productive manner, and hopefully conjoint problem solving can occur.

What can you do to keep strong and cool, and to see your loved one's point of view while maintaining your own personal sense of integrity and self-worth? How can you use I messages when discussing critical events to avoid hostility?

It Takes A Long Time To Eat Humble Pie
From The Speed Of Light
To The Speed Of Mind

> *To err is human, forgive divine.*
> **William Shakespeare**

Loved ones who have taken care of veterans over time burnout. Burnout occurs because all people are rate limited; they can only care and give so much. Many times when a combat veteran who has had difficulty coping emotionally and has been angry, caustic, bitter, and withdrawn starts to feel better, attempting to be less angry, even more social, loved ones still seem angry, even short tempered themselves.

Those exposed to combat veterans with post traumatic stress disorders often develop a form of stress disorder themselves. This is secondary PTSD. Secondary PTSD can be thought of as a reflection, the mirror image of PTSD. The problem, however, is this reflection is not instant, in the moment, but rather a reflection in the mind.

Light travels at one hundred eighty-six thousand miles per second, and the mind handles information at ninety-three feet per second. Just as a combat veteran has learned that certain cues in the environment may trigger trouble, those around and exposed to the combat veteran have learned to look for cues in the veteran which may mean signs of trouble.

Loved ones may feel cranky and irritable themselves, and the veteran feels perplexed not knowing why his spouse or loved ones, children, or family members seem distant and cranky.

It takes a long time to eat humble pie. When the combat veteran realizes that anger has been displaced on family members and loved ones, and begins to make changes, it is not surprising that loved ones, particularly those with their own secondary PTSD, do not automatically applaud or notice the veteran's effort.

Why is this? This occurs partly because there are still conditioned triggers which the veteran is displaying which lead to a level of arousal in our loved ones. The second is that our loved ones have learned that when you are feeling better and more genial, it is their opportunity to vent.

When this occurs, remember, **it takes a long time to eat humble pie,** and that when venting occurs it is time to de-escalate the tension, and to remind yourself to err is human, and forgive divine.

The Ten Thousand Meter Stare:
Doctor My Eyes

Doctor my eyes,
have seen the years,
and the slow parade of fears,
without crying.
Now I want to understand.

I have done all that I could
to see the evil and the good,
without hiding.
You must help me if you can.

Doctor in my eyes,
tell me what is wrong.
Was I unwise,
to leave them open for so long?

As I have wandered through this world
as each moment has unfurled,
I have been waiting
to awaken from these dreams,

People go just where they will
I never noticed them until,
I got this feeling that its later than it seemed.

Doctor in my eyes,
tell me what you see.
I hear their cries.
Just say if it's too late for me.

Doctor in my eyes,
I can not see the sky.
Is this the price,
for having learned how not to cry.

Jackson Browne

Have you ever been accused of having that stare, that look in your eyes, the one that can scare? You probably saw it in other veterans while in the war zone, and now are you aware that you may have that stare, but this time it is your own.

Why is this? Where does this look come from? And, why is this so unsettling, so unseemly to others?

Everything we see and hear is initially processed by the primitive part of our brain, our dinosaur brain. We have specific triggers that we have learned are the sounds, sights, and smells of danger.

When we react with an edge, the low level of anger, hypervigilance, and dread, we have that stare, that glare, that scares.

Certain triggers are hard wired. They are ingrained within us. They are inherited from our own biological history. We all can identify a mad dog by its glare, its growl, and so it seems that the ten thousand meter stare, which you share in times of despair, is such a trigger to those for whom you care.

Knowing this, and owning this, what can you do to comfort your loved ones and avert this look so easily mistook?

Cues Of Safety
Living Life In The Here And The Now
It's OK To Be OK

A post traumatic stress disorder is an anxiety disorder. Anxiety is a feeling of worry about the future. The basic ingredient of all anxiety disorders is that there is an overuse of usual survival mechanisms. **A combat veteran will over respond to his environment which leads to excessive or incorrectly activated defense mechanisms.**

These mechanisms which are incorrectly activated occur automatically without much forethought. There is an issue of negative transfer where previous learning in a war-time experience leaves the combat veteran applying past learning, that was essential for survival, in meeting the demands of a current situation.

Part of this basic response system consists of stinkin' thinkin' or wearisome worrying which leads to decision making so quickly that it tends to be over inclusive and not sufficiently discriminating in order to understand that the cues or triggers are not truly threats at all. Before the combat veteran can conceptualize the moment accurately physiological reactions that are automatic occur and, in most cases, when an arousal reaction or wild ride happens the combat veteran has

not correctly distinguished between true physical danger or psychosocial threat and what is simply a nuisance and an inconvenience.

Combat veterans will over estimate risks and magnitude of perceived
danger.

**We can't change the past. We can only help along the future by
learning to manage the moment.** The truth is **we live life in the here
and in the now,** and it is only within a moment, that brief perception of
time, that we are truly able to make a correction. You might ask yourself
in the here and in the now: What are you aware of in your own
thoughts, feelings, bodily sensations? Are you making an accurate
assessment of the harm; physical harm, social harm? Are you able to
provide other strategies to relable what appears to be a misperception
using logic dampening the impact of stinkin' thinkin' and wearisome
worrying?

One trick is to learn to identify cues of safety, and begin relying on
these cues as evidence that there is no threat of danger.

What are your cues of safety? How can you distinguish between
physical threat and psychosocial threat? How can you relable difficulties
in your environment as being a nuisance and an inconvenience rather
than something that is awful or terrible? What is the difference?

Many times, combat veterans, because they overreact and utilize
excessively survival mechanisms, begin to feel less worthwhile. In the
here and now, the combat veteran may dwell upon their own shortcomings for overreacting. Others may see the veteran as chronically irritable, isolated, or grumpy. The veteran hears this from loved ones and
feels badly, sad, and depressed. What can you do to reinforce searching
out your own cues for safety? What can you do to remind yourself that
it is OK for you to be OK? You don't always have to be your own worst
critic. It is not now necessary for survival. Take the time to nurture
yourself and become a true friend to a body and mind that has learned
not to protect your soul but rather ensure your survival.

It's OK For Things To Be OK

Give us this day our 'Daily Dread,' and forgive us our trespasses
as we forgive those whom we believe
are about to trespass against us.

Harrison Prawl

Many combat veterans find that they wake up with a sense of dread or foreboding. This expectation for harm or apprehension greets them every morning prior to beginning their day. Often combat veterans feel anxious about what may happen, and know that they begin to feel better once they are out and about dealing with their daily responsibilities.

Psychologists who study systems, family systems, small group systems, note that dysfunctional systems have a tendency to focus on **an identified problem.** This **dysfunctional focus** allows the system, family or small group, to focus their energies on an identified problem, and this provides a sense of balance to the system.

Combat veterans often find themselves seeking a dysfunctional focus. You might find yourself searching for the next identifiable difficulty or problem. As you reflect now, what are the sources of your own dysfunctional focus? Where do you put blame: on others, the Veterans Administration, Social Security Administration, family members, wife, children, or, do you find a dysfunctional focus on aspects of yourself?

Psychologists who study systems, both systems within individuals themselves as well as small groups and larger group interactions, note that in dysfunctional individuals and in dysfunctional systems that a **dysfunctional focus** is critical for that system to maintain and sustain itself.

One difficulty in getting better is that the system, whether it be within the individual or within a group or organization, has learned to rely on a dysfunctional focus. This dysfunctional focus provides a vortex, a central point in which other aspects of the self, small group or organization, can point a finger and revolve around.

When this vortex, this central point, is eliminated or problem is taken care of many times individuals and/or systems have difficulty finding a new balance.

As you take stock of your own progress and achieve another goal, you are likely to find yourself experiencing a sense of dread and anxiety. This apprehension or expectation for harm should be relabled as a central component of a post traumatic stress disorder. This dread can serve as a cue for self validation.

It is extremely important to learn to live with a sense of homeostasis, or balance, and to be aware that you are in a clear and safe space.

When you have reached the clear space it is important to remind yourself, even though you have a sense of dread and an expectation for harm, that it is **OK for things to be OK.**

Many times combat veterans have learned that there is quiet before a storm, a firefight, or a battle, and this quiet can be a trigger for arousal. **It is important to catch these moments of tranquillity and, not allow them to become a trigger, reminding yourself again that it is OK for things to be OK.**

Down In The Valley And The Cumulative Effects Of Traumatic Exposure

Success means trying one more time.

Thomas A. Edison

When the text *Trauma and the Vietnam War Generation* which was published in 1990, the findings indicated that of the 3.14 million men who served in-country in Vietnam, one-fourth were at that time currently suffering some degree of a post traumatic stress disorder. Fifteen percent of Vietnam veterans suffered from full blown post traumatic stress disorders. These numbers, to a greater degree, appear to be consistent with other numbers from other conflicts. The summary of the literature indicates that approximately fifteen percent of combat veterans suffer from full blown post traumatic stress disorders while another fifteen percent at any one time may suffer periodic symptoms of a post traumatic stress disorder which are so incapacitating to significantly interfere with the quality of one's life affecting intimacy in personal relationships, and maintaining and sustaining employment, for example. Other evidence indicates that the longer one is exposed to combat and the more intense the combat is, the more likely one is to suffer the psychiatric consequences of that combat.

Psychiatric casualties accounted for fifty percent of personnel loss during the 8th Air Force's bombing of Europe, and fifty percent of casualties during the Battle of Okinawa were also psychiatric. In most instances these were not cases where individuals refused to fight, but rather were judged by peers and superiors as no longer being effective.

There appears to be cumulative effects of trauma. A history of an abusive childhood is likely to increase the probability that later combat exposure will lead to post traumatic stress disorder characteristics. Veterans who take positions of responsibility in work following combat exposure where they are exposed to trauma as firefighter, policeman, or emergency service personnel increase the likelihood that they too will experience full blown post traumatic stress disorders.

Over a period of time snapshots, or flashbulb memories of trauma build up and eventually overwhelm an individual's ability to cope. Primary characteristics of a post traumatic stress disorder include exposure to a traumatic event. Traumatic events that appear to be humanly caused as opposed to natural disasters such floods, tornadoes, and hurricanes are much more devastating. The development of an expectation for harm or dread, chronic anger, a tendency to want to isolate oneself, to control as much of one's environment as possible, to feel uncomfortable in groups of people and more comfortable when one's back is to the wall, along with marked startle reaction, hypervigilance, and intrusive memories of one's traumatic experience or combat exposure are cardinal characteristics of a post traumatic stress disorder. Secondary problems to a post traumatic stress disorder include depression, a sense of worthlessness, a lack of energy, and, at times, severe periods of anxiety which can last for several days and which are extremely uncomfortable.

Many times veterans begin receiving care when their world has fallen down upon them like a house of cards, and everything that one has worked for and strived for has been threatened, challenged, or has

been lost. Many times a combat veteran may ask, why me? Is this a sign of personal weakness? Do I really have such a disorder or problem? When a full blown post traumatic stress disorder occurs, many times the veteran has managed to hit bottom or finds oneself **deep in the valley or in the trough.**

The **trough** is a metaphor and can be seen as deep with walls. The veteran feels incapable of climbing out on one's own without a sense of validation that one is worthwhile, important, or one's service matters. It is very lonely and very frustrating to be on the bottom and in the trough. Feelings of hopelessness and despair are likely to occur.

Veterans often begin the search for compensation as well as assistance when they have managed to discover themselves at the bottom of this trough, and it is a slow process finding a way out. Many times to get out of the trough requires a helping hand from peers, friends, and professionals willing to offer such help and assistance.

Thomas Edison, the inventor of so many of our appliances including the electric light, phonograph, and the motion picture, states that he probably tried over one hundred thousand combinations before he was able to develop a light bulb, and stated that for him, success meant "trying one more time."

It is important never to give up. It takes once to quit, and quitting is easy. Everyone who is successful has failed, and everyone who is successful has tried again. When you are in the trough and lack the energy, sometimes it is helpful to see that others have managed to climb, crawl, and be helped out of the trough. The lack of validation one receives when you are turned down by the Veterans Administration for compensation is devastating, but it is only through persistence and through documentation that you will begin to understand the components and the cumulative effects of a post traumatic stress disorder and can begin the journey out of the valley.

What steps have you taken currently to help yourself move out of the trough, or out of the valley? If you have been able to move beyond this, what have you done to provide peer support to other veterans who are now where you once were?

Lessons Not Learned Are Repeated
And The Art Of Reframing

We have come out of the time when obedience,
the acceptance of discipline, intelligent courage,
and resolution were most important,
into that more difficult time when it is a man's duty
to understand his world rather than simply fight for it.

Ernest Hemmingway

What is right? How can we live our lives with dignity and honor and be true to ourselves and our own family? Often, combat veterans carry with them a sense of anger which interferes with their ability to successfully cope with day to day demands or, in particular, more complicated demands.

Because we have the ability to understand right and wrong, and morality at the most highest level, we are often perplexed and have feelings of despair because we are troubled by the thoughts that we have which may truly be the most dangerous in our own mind.

For the most part, however, those most aggressive thoughts are put away and expressed in an off handed manner. We may choose to deny problems, avoid problems, isolate ourselves from others, not communicate our thoughts and feelings, and somehow find a pet method for coping. Over a period of time these natural defenses can create difficulties and shortcomings, and, because of this, **lessons not learned are repeated.**

As you take the time now to examine repetitive difficulties in your own life, how can these be formed as a lesson? What have you learned about yourself? What difficulties are repeated time and time and time again? Are these really a common problem or are they critical difficulties which deserve a plan?

As we reflect on our own traumatic histories and experiences and do so in a safe and secure environment, it allows us to become in touch with those memories, some vivid, some unpleasant, some difficult to recall, and understand now with greater insight what it was to be a young man facing combat filled with a sense of purpose, perhaps initially, and later to feel disenfranchised because of one's combat experience, and wondering now: **How can I as a combat veteran reframe my experience in the aftermath of my service from a perspective that has meaning?**

Ernest Hemmingway cautions us that it is more important to understand the world rather than simply fight for it. It is important to understand who we are as people; that we have a need for nurturance. We have a need for love; that we are social beings; and that we can misperceive other cultures, people—even people within our own country—whose skin is different, whose religions are different, whose cultural values are different, and, in that sense, make them our enemy.

When we take a look at the lessons of life and those that are repeated seeing these lessons are an opportunity for change, for constructive change, and turn a repeating disappointment into a plan, then hope is possible. This hope and this self understanding assists in reframing past traumatic events and current ongoing trauma, allowing the veteran to live their life with a sense of purpose and dignity. It is through this that change and renewal are possible, and change and renewal are the essence and the bounty of hope.

Boxes And Mirrors

And in the end the love you take is equal to the love you make.
Lennon and McCartney

In the last seventy years American society has changed and much of our human social interactions have become artificial. In the past seventy years our nation, once primarily agricultural, has become industrial and now technological and service oriented. Families have shrunk from an extended family unit to nuclear families of two generations to what some refer to as atomic families of single parent households or blended families.

George Carlin, a popular comedian who looks at life and language, describes people as living in and separated from others by our boxes. He tells us that houses are not homes but rather just big boxes to hold our stuff. We travel from box to box or work to home in the box with wheels. Now, at work many people interact with a box during their work day, and this box is a computer, only to again ride in their wheeled box to their box of stuff. At home the people who might be in the stuff box are separated by cubicles or walls, and rather than interacting with each other the people who live in the stuff box spend their time looking at pretend life occurring in a little box, a TV, or interact with their own home computer which is just another box.

Those psychologists who study our species understand that people are social beings. We have a need for social contact. Psychologists who study veterans note that those with combat post traumatic stress disorders have an avoidance of many social interactions. Now, society limits our interaction with others. Many people are unable to fulfill their own social needs because of the social constraints society has placed on itself. Combat veterans understand well that people are the most dangerous aspect or animal on this planet, and their natural tendency to avoid social interaction, particularly those social interactions which are ambiguous or not clear in nature, only exacerbates this problem.

As a combat veteran you may ask yourself whether you avoid social interactions, what social interactions will you participate in, and what circumstances would be minimally acceptable for you to participate? What feelings do you have regarding people in general, your community in general, and mankind?

We have discussed before that a component central to combat PTSD is an underlying level of anger and frustration. How do you see the people around you now? What feelings and emotions do you see in significant others? **The actions and behaviors you see in those around you are a reflection of yourself.** Look at those around you understanding that what you see in the people closest to you is just a reflection of your own internal state. **What do you see in this mirror reflecting back at you?**

The truth is the people that surround us are a reflection of who we are.

To live a life worth living, a life that is rewarding, making an art out of living, begins with giving, loving, and sharing. It is only when this concept is mastered will those surrounding you begin to reflect a more positive quality.

What can you do to nurture the relationships around you in order to seek a more fulfilling personal life? How have the problems of our society, being a combatant, and your own personal apprehension and dread interfered with your ability to find love and intimacy? What can you do to overcome these obstacles?

The Problem Of Violence
From Frustration To Aggression

And let no one say that violence is the courageous way,
that violence is the short route, that violence is the easy route.
Because violence will bring no answer; It will bring no answer...

Robert F. Kennedy

Bobby Kennedy spoke these words the evening of Martin Luther King's assassination in April 1968. He was speaking to a group of African-American leaders in Indianapolis, Indiana. During this speech, he also stated that if we learned anything from the '60s, it was that violence was not the answer to our problems or society's problems.

For a combat veteran, you were trained in the art, skill, even science of warfare, organized violence. The problem now is within your mind when the rage rises to its surface and anger crosses that threshold, that violence is envisioned and this vision is a terrifying one. **Trained for war, yet not trained for peace is a difficulty mostly combat veterans face.**

Many combat veterans have learned that they are more afraid of themselves and their own actions rather than the actions of others. But intrusive thoughts, thoughts of violent acts to deal with life's frustrations can plague the veteran.

Much of violence is learned. We learn to act violently in one's preparation for combat in training, but violence is also exacerbated by a media which attends and stores acts of violence like a cauldron contained on television, radio, and the printed page.

Social psychologists have observed that violence could be modeled and learned from watching the interactions of others as well as television, cartoons, movies, and the media.

Social psychologists have shown that **frustration leads to aggression.** Frustration is an emotion defined as an inability in obtaining one's goals, or not achieving one's wants and needs. As a veteran, have you ever found yourself beginning to feel angry because you are not achieving a goal, that this goal leads to feelings of frustration, and frustration to acting out, even violently?

Are you aware that you have modeled or displayed to your family members, peers, and co-workers your anger, and that anger can fuel aggressive and violent acts, words and deeds toward any among those you love the most?

We know that intrusive thoughts, thoughts of violence or bad thoughts, lead to bad feelings, and bad feelings lead to bad emotions, and bad emotions to a physiological change in the body that can result in rage and acts of violence.

We also know as combat veterans that a sense of precaution and vigilance is helpful at staving off underlying feelings of anxiety. There is a difference between prudence and caution and anger, however. This prudence and caution can be an edge, an edge of protection against vulnerability.

What steps have you taken to reframe your own natural tendencies to contemplate acts of violence. Thoughts of violence are likely to evoke feelings of shame or guilt. How have you caught yourself with such a feeling and reminded yourself that only good people feel guilty, and that the truth is that **violence is taught and violence is learned** by the behavior of others around you, carried on and handed down to others?

Those scientists who study the beginning of people have noted that the history of warfare is just ten thousand years old. It begins with our history of civilization. Before man lived in society we apparently did not war on each other. But once we had things, stuff, and possessions, wants and needs beget violence. In order to protect society from violence we have harnessed the energy of our species organizing in armies and navies and airforces and police to combat other societies, groups, gangs, and individuals who engage in acts of violence.

What can you do as a combat veteran to set aside violence as a tool to live your life peacefully and to be content with yourself, your family, and community?

Flashbulb Memories And Flashbacks
From Feelings To Emotions

We all experience **flashbulb memories.** But combat veterans sometimes experience **flashbacks** of their combat experiences or distortions of perception in which they interpret the environment as being a scene from one's wartime past. **Flashbulb memories are just snapshots,** and we all have very vivid pictures in our mind. We can reflect and probably recall the first and earliest memories or the first time you saw and met your wife. These are very vivid pictures that do not necessarily lead to another scene or a series of pictures. **Flashbacks occur when we see, hear, or smell triggers in the environment which lead to more than a flashbulb or snapshot memory, but rather to a production, MGM Presents, for example, and in our mind's eye we vividly relive a combat experience or see the world that we are in, in the here and now, as if it were somewhere in the combat zone.**

An emotion is more than a feeling. An emotion is a stronger reaction which involves a feeling. A feeling such as happy, sad, mad, or glad, does not necessarily involve a physiological change occurring within the body. An emotion involves a feeling plus a physiological reaction in the body. **Flashbulb memories do not necessarily evoke an emotion. Flashbacks, however, almost uniformly do involve a very strong physiological response in which adrenaline and other chemicals are manufactured. We** know that with flashbacks adrenaline is produced, sugar is released, heart rate increases, blood pressure increases, we may sweat, and feelings of anger, rage, and terror may ensue. During a flashback visual images can move from one's mind's eye to being in your visual field in the here and now. When this change occurs, typically, individuals move within a disso-ciative state in which their experiences become disconnected from the reality that others perceive. Combat veterans who frequently experience flashbacks often have dissociative states in which common perception of reality remains distorted to the point that one's sense of consciousness about the here and now becomes lost. When this occurs an individual will feel as if they have simply lost time.

When reflecting on your own history you are surely aware of your own flashbulb memories, good times and bad, and you may also have had experiences of flashing and/or physiologically reacting and emot-ing rather than just having feelings and visual memories. What coping skills are you using to minimize flashbulb memories and prevent flash-backs from occurring. What sights, sounds, and smells trigger for you these experiences? What coping skills have you used? How have you shared you understanding of this with your loved ones?

Scientists who study the evolution of the brain, neurologists and neuropsychologists, have found that sights and sounds trigger more primitive parts of the brain, but smells seem to evoke an even stronger response. Why is this? It appears that our smart brain, our cerebral cor-tex, has developed from our olfactory, our smelling part of the brain. Smells, then, can be even more significant triggers and stimuli for flash-bulb memories and potential flashbacks. Knowing the distinction between feelings and emotions, how can you recognize your own trig-gers, recognize your own feelings, and attempt to reduce the probability of an emotional reaction and the debilitating effects of dissociation which occurs during a true flashback?

Slip Sliding Away:
The Nature Of Dissociative Processes

Slip sliding away
Slip sliding away
The nearer your destination
The more you keep slip sliding away.

Paul Simon

Psychological numbing to traumatic events is one of the immediate reactions to a severely stressful event. Such psychological numbing immediately following a traumatic event should be seen, in part, as adaptive. **Becoming numb to traumatic exposure, the individual is able to carry on, but in a diminished capacity.** Why is this? What is happening? And, how psychologically numbing presents itself as dissociative phenomena is important for combat veterans to understand.

Dissociation results in reduced responsiveness to one's environment. It is a way for the individual to invalidate one's immediate environment. Biologically, a dissociative phenomena can be occur because of : 1) a brain disorder such as specific injury to the brain or temporal lobe dysfunction; 2) substance abuse; 3) and, most importantly for combat veterans, extreme stress or trauma.

Dissociative experiences include: depersonalization, derealization, fugue states, and amnesia.

Biologically, we know that combat veterans have trouble with short term memory, specifically, because of damage to the hippocampus and the ongoing working memory. There is a tendency to lateralize or to have a heightened level of experience in one's right or visual spatial brain rather than left smart brain which reduces one's language functioning.

You may appear to others as forgetful, not tuned in, distant, difficulty expressing yourself, dysfluent, and under extreme episodes of dissociation you will loose time, anywhere from a few moments to a few days. You may appear to others as if you are intoxicated even though you are not. Why is this?

Poor gross motor coordination is associated with dissociative behavior because of an increase in right brain activity which is responsible for visual and spatial relationships. Difficulty operating a motor vehicle and traffic accidents are often noted when individuals are having increased dissociative episodes. **Flashbacks are part of dissociative experiences.**

Everything from short term memory loss to a feeling of being clumsy to word finding difficulty, and feeling estranged are all concomitants of dissociation. This tendency to slip slide away should just be a cue to utilize coping skills. Remember, if you feel yourself slip sliding away, this is a behavior or cue for you to begin utilizing your bag of tricks.

The primary function of dissociative phenomenon is to provide you with a method of regulating exposure to harmful cues related to your traumatic experience. Something has happened and triggered this reaction. Cues can be obvious such as loud noises, certain smells, times of the year, anniversary dates, weather conditions, and crowded places.

Dissociation is a natural but harmful method for regulating an exposure to trauma. It is a process and a state that will pass.

Anger Displacement
And The Anger Thermometer

Anger is a feeling, and it is an emotion. When we experience **anger** we may express it to others. We may focus our **anger** on other people, circumstances, situations, or institutions, or we may swallow the **anger** whole. The truth, however, is that anger is usually not an instant emotional reaction, but rather, builds.

Psychologists who study the development of people and those psychologists who study comparative psychology exploring how people differ from other animals, primarily other mammals, note that in development animals and children usually begin their lives experiencing pleasure, displeasure, pain, and satisfaction. When this displeasure and pain grow to an intense level, anger is expressed. **Anger, then, can grow further into a rage.**

While some may say that it is helpful to express one's anger, anyone who is truly angry is out of control. When you look back at your own times of being angry, you realize that you too were out of control. Anger involves subcortical processing of those primitive parts of the brain, of the dinosaur brain. It involves such structures such as the amyglada or the limbic system. When we are truly angry, adrenaline is produced that leads to a fight/flight phenomenon.

Displacement occurs when we take our anger, irritation, and hurt feelings out on others. This is a psychological defense and it is a harmful defense. Emotions, ideas, or wishes are transferred from an original object to more acceptable substitutes. This usually is used to allay anxiety. We may become angry because a cabinet door is left ajar, or a lid is stuck on a jelly jar, or traffic lines are too long. In these instances a substitute becomes the focal point of built up anger and the anger is displaced. Coming home from a difficult day at the office and kicking the cat would be an example of displacement. Unfortunately, for many combat veterans displacement is often focused on those who love and care for us the most.

A central component to combat PTSD is lingering feelings of anger. However, if we pay attention to ourselves we will note that this anger usually builds by a combination of stinkin' thinkin' or dysfunctional thoughts or inappropriate conclusions we are making about the world around us. **It is helpful to imagine a thermometer.** At the lowest level of this mood thermometer might be the edge followed by irritability, frustrated, pissed, mad, and above that when we begin experiencing that adrenaline rush or wild ride, anger, and rage.

Combat veterans frequently find it easier to hold on to a low level of irritability we refer to as the edge. This edge gives one a sense of security and avoids a feeling of vulnerability. It is only through practice, use of relaxation techniques, and finding one's clear or safe space that it is possible to let go of the anger, pass through a period of vulnerability, and feel secure.

What skills have you found are helpful in stopping yourself from escalating from mad to angry and avoiding a rage reaction?

Psychologist's have noted that **any time someone is angry** with another situation, institution, or organization **they truly are not free because that circumstance or object of anger owns them.** It is only when a combat veteran has learned to reduce their level of anger to this low edge and pass through feelings of vulnerability can they truly find happiness, contentment, and enjoyment in life.

Once A Warrior Always A Worrier,
Yet A Gentleman

Stinkin' Thinkin' and the feeling of dread, apprehension, and an expectation for harm are all central components to a post traumatic stress disorder. This ongoing dialogue of worry and fret appears to be characteristic of individuals who have served in combat. Why is this? Expecting harm, and planning for all contingencies provides a sense of safety and security. Thinking about the short term consequences and long term consequences of one's actions and coming up with a plan to deal with both short and long term consequences helps to provide a sense of security. But for combat veterans, typically, this tendency to worry can become an encumbrance, a hindrance on living spontaneously and enjoying life.

Have your loved ones or significant others ever complained because you fret too much? Have you expressed anger and frustration because of what if's and what might happen?

Anxiety is the difference between what is happening right now in this moment and what will happen in the future. Anticipating and worrying about the future with thoughts flow with this feeling of anxiety, dread, or apprehension. Frustration is a feeling that individuals have when they fail to meet a goal and, many times, for combat veterans, trying to specify the nature of the worries or dread makes a goal less obscure.

One goal, a simple one, is finding a safe space, a clear space, one free from a sense of vulnerability or free from being overwhelmed.

What can be done to cope with this natural tendency to worry? One method to cope is to look at what you know about a situation in the first place, and learn how to manage the moment. What is happening in the here and right now? Secondly, the trick is to learn to help others feel as comfortable and as safe as you would like to feel yourself.

One definition of a gentleman is that **a gentleman tries to make others feel as comfortable as he feels or would like to feel.** Such an individual will be seen as courteous and gracious with a strong sense of honor. Placing the focus on others around you or externalizing your focus, you feel more comfortable. By being courteous and gracious, and conducting yourself with a sense of honor, you can give yourself a sense of validation which reduces the possibility of tedious worry and nettlesome thinking.

Taking Stock Of Your Progress
And The Problem With Hope

Has there ever been a time when you have climbed a mountain or a hill and stood for a moment on the highest peak or point around? Have you looked down on earth and the terrain below with nothing above you but a canopy of sky and clouds? If you reflect, what did it take you to arrive at that point and at that moment? If you ponder on that moment and in your circumspection relive what it took for you to achieve that vantage and grasp that view, what did it take to struggle against the mountain? What effort was required to lift yourself above the horizon, and what did you learn about yourself for having taken the time and the effort just for that view? In the end we always learn something about ourselves when we conquer a mountain. **When we conquer other life's difficulties we end up learning something about ourselves as well.**

In understanding a post traumatic stress disorder, learning the biological components, the events which for you have precipitated the hypervigilance, the arousal, the marked startle response, and intrusive memories, and now in climbing and overcoming the limitations of a post traumatic stress disorder, what have you learned about yourself?

In reviewing what you have learned about yourself, you must take stock of your own progress. It is important to take a look at where you were when you began this journey. It is important to compare where you are now with where you have been, not where others are at. It is important to compete with yourself not with others, and it is necessary to learn from others who are a little further along and to help others who follow or are behind. What have you learned from other veterans who have gained greater insight than you now have? And, what can you offer others who are beginning this journey?

One component of a post traumatic stress disorder is a sense of dread or apprehension which unchecked becomes hypervigilance and an expectation for harm. **Beginning a journey to conquer PTSD starts with an expectation of success:** To understand that a post traumatic stress disorder is a manageable condition and that the quality of one's life will surely improve with effort.

The beginning of this journey and the maintenance of this journey is based on **hope. Hope** carries with it an expectation of success or better-ment, but the **problem with hope** is that there is an understanding that one's journey may not be successful.

Having hope is a good thing, and hope is a realistic and a good feeling. To understand that there are problems ahead, problems to be dealt with, planned for, and overcome is all part of hope. With hope comes prudence, caution, and good planning. Hope is an understanding that things may not work out, but with effort and determination you will be able to climb this mountain. You will be able to succeed, and you will be able to improve the quality of your life and the lives of those who are significant to you.

As you reflect now, what are your **hopes**? What are the impediments to success? What are you cautious and prudent about? And, how can you make a plan to achieve your own **hopes** and dreams?

Turn A Difficulty Into A Plan
Don't Turn A Difficulty Into A Problem

*The initiation of any scientific inquiry must first begin with
a circumspection of that which we know about
the subject in the first place.*

Burtrand Russell

Burtrand Russell, a philosopher of science, provides an excellent clue for us in problem solving. Combat veterans frequently experience a fight/flight phenomena. Usually this is in response to specific difficulties which have led to an adrenaline, or dinosaur dump, placing the individual on a wild ride. It is important to realize that planning is the most proactive method of fighting. As you gain skills in coping, reducing the probability that you are having an adrenaline dump, it is still important to utilize good problem solving skills.

The trick is to **turn a difficulty into a plan and not turn that difficulty into a problem.** Difficulties usually occur because we feel frustrated and we are unable to achieve certain goals. When looking at a difficulty, **the most important thing is to first remain external rather than internal in viewing the situation.**

It is important to understand the details of any difficulty first: What are the facts? What are the components? What is the nature of that difficulty? We must ask ourselves first, what do we understand about the difficulty? Whether it be in our interpersonal relations with others, a job, pursuit of compensation, or in dealing with usual reoccurring triggers in the environment which may lead to arousal. As you read this you are probably aware in your own mind of some of your own difficulties. You may stop now and ask, what do I really understand about this now? What are the components? What are the facts?

Once you have looked at these components externally, then it is OK to look at what you know about yourself and how you interpret the world. Individuals with combat PTSD typically begin each day with the feeling of dread, apprehension, an expectation for harm, and a belief that things are not going to work out. There is a tendency to taint our perception of external events. By taking the time to reframe your own natural tendency to look at the world with such dread, you allow yourself to put the difficulty into perspective.

Developing a plan usually occurs spontaneously when you have had an opportunity to examine the facts, first externally and then internally. The best plans are usually creative ones which balance the needs between external and internal issues. As you think about your difficulties after having examined components of the problem, are solutions readily apparent or do you need time to let aspects of this difficulty percolate? If a problem can not be solved immediately through principles of assimilation into preexisting problem strategies, then the mind must accommodate, make new structures, and make new associations. Accommodation typically comes through insight, and this generally requires some time.

In doing so **it is important not to turn a difficulty into a problem and not overreact.** Has anyone ever accused you of reacting before thinking, or a loved one pointed out that you blunder through uncomfortable situations in a need and attempt to control things immediately? Patience is a virtue that is acquired through practice, and the heart of patience is understanding that you have a plan to deal with difficulties.

Even when you are in the midst of a wild ride and extremely uncomfortable, simply telling yourself that you have a plan, that you understand what is going on externally, that you have a sense of what is going on internally, can help quiet the rage within and help tame the anger. This is because planning is one of the most proactive ways of fighting and dealing with this flight/flight phenomena.

The Moral Animal

*To every thing there is a season, and a time to
every purpose under the heaven.
A time to be born, and a time to die; a time to
plant, and a time to pluck up that which is planted;
A time to kill, and a time to heal; a time to break
down, and a time to build up;
A time to weep, and a time to laugh; a time to
mourn, and a time to dance;
A time to cast away stones, and a time to gather
stones together; a time to embrace, and a time to
refrain from embracing;
A time to get, and a time to lose; a time to keep,
and a time to cast away;
A time to rend, and a time to sew; a time to keep
silence, and a time to speak;
A time to love, and a time to hate; a time of war,
and a time of peace.*

Ecclesiastes 3:1-8

Human beings are the only species believed to have the ability to
reason with a sense of morality. As a combat veteran you have been

exposed to specific trauma and incidents which have challenged your sense of right and wrong.

Our law is ultimately based on a perception and understanding of a higher law. What is true, what is right, and what is just is codified in legal statutes and lawful orders, but what is morally right may at times be different than what is prescribed by law.

As a soldier you are asked to defend your country, and in so doing set aside some of your moral teachings that you learned as a child or young adult.

How have the experiences you have participated in affected your sense of morality? With this understanding, how can you live your life with a sense of morality?

Rules Of Engagement

All's fair in love and war.
Francis Edward Smedley

As a combat veteran you were subject to the rules of engagement. These rules of engagement specified how, when, where, and to what extent you could engage the enemy in hostile action. The saying, "all's fair in love and war," is not true. The truth about this saying is that it can explain away or make honorable uncivilized acts in primary relationships. But in war, war conducted by a civilized nation with civilized soldiers acting on the direction of a democratically elected president and congress, there are rules. **The problem many combatants faced in the field was that these rules intensified the precarious nature of war and increased the combatants' vulnerability.**

A soldier, sailor, marine, or airman in the field individually representing the political and military goals of his country, is a target, by placing himself in harm's way. The combatant presents himself to be slain.

Douglas McArthur stated that the epitome of civilization was that lone combatant moving forward headlong into hostile, enemy fire. For a young man to set aside all his hopes, dreams, wants, and needs for a higher purpose, was the summit of a civilization.

But individual combatants do not experience war on some broad philosophical level. Combatants experience war in the here and now, in extremes of physical fear, fatigue, exhilaration, the extremes of temperatures, inadequate meals and other forms of physical stress.

Rules of engagement can subject the combatant to an increased level of vulnerability. Because of this, there is an opportunity for psychopaths to come to dominate both formal and informal power structures in a combat setting.

Under the extreme tug of life and death, unprincipled individuals who lack personal rules of engagement and civility, who are character disordered, can impose their own informal structure on those around them. It is within this environment that atrocity can occur. This occurs because there is, in the heat of combat, an absence of law and order and usual moral constraints which guide our actions.

What is right and wrong and what is moral has been challenged. An individual combatant may be told by a chaplain that he is on a crusade, and the act of taking life in military action is just and moral, and the act is not murder but an act of warfare.

The line between right and wrong becomes blurred with a need for survival and safety. At the end of one's combat exposure many veterans have seen and witnessed acts that they are uncertain about morally, and they feel tainted, soiled and dirty because of this.

The truth is, only the good feel guilty. But the problem is, the good then lack self-confidence and a sense of self-worth, and the good then feel that they are not worthy of a life worth living.

As you reflect now on the rules of engagement which guided your actions in combat you may question how those rules of engagement affect you now. Is there a sense of mistrust and betrayal because the rules were unjust and unfair? How have these rules of engagement affected you and your family now? If you do feel dirty and tainted by your experience, it is important to remind yourself that only the good feel guilty. Further, as you look back on your life since combat and are ashamed somehow of overreacting or not responding in a civilized manner, understand this: **When you recognize your behavior in the past as shameful, this is now a sign of personal maturity and growth. Take homage.**

Sublimation And The Trouble
With Too Much Introspection

An unexamined life is not worth living.

Socrates

As a combat veteran, perhaps the healthiest psychological defense is sublimation. Sublimation refers to channeling one's psychic or psychological energy into productive activities. An example could be restoring a motorcycle, working in a garden, trimming one's roses, helping make repairs to your home, assisting a friend, fishing with or socializing with family.

While Socrates concluded, "an unexamined life is not worth living," too much introspection or rather self-examination is not healthy. It is productive to have a planning time during the day to reflect on your goals, where you are at, and where you would like to be. But to mull over your troubles all day long is not healthy, it leads to stinkin' thinkin', should, oughts or musts, musterbation.

What activities, hobbies, interests, have you used to channel your energy? and, how have you developed positive problem solving for yourself? If you are not doing these activities, how can you begin?

Have you found the power of piddling? Do your loved ones understand how helpful these activities are for your peace of mind?

Immature Psychological Defense Mechanisms

The lives of ordinary men are spent in days of quiet desperation.

Gregory Bateson

There are three groups of common psychological defenses which can be described as 1) immature, 2) common neurotic or defenses of safety, and 3) mature psychological defenses or defenses of helping and healing.

For combat veterans, these psychological defenses are primarily designed to maintain the survivability or integrity of the individual. The most primitive of this group or immature psychological defenses have their roots in anger, dread, and in an expectation for harm.

Many combat veterans report that when it is too quiet they feel anxious. As a consequence, before one has gained acceptance of combat PTSD, individuals are likely to develop a primitive method of psychological defense consisting of either blaming, complaining, or procrastinating.

A defense of blaming, or tilting at windmills, consists of a combat veteran needing to find a focus for anger and irritability. Having an identified problem or dysfunctional focus allows the veteran to challenge his uncomfortable and unresolved anger.

Tilting at windmills comes from Cervante's, Don Quixote. In this novel, an aging knight whose eye sight is poor finds himself out of place and out of touch with changes in society and misperceives a windmill in a distance as a knight with lance. If you find yourself angry and having a need to focus or blame, you might ask yourself if you too are tilting at windmills seeking a confrontation in order to discharge or displace unfinished business from one's own combat history.

A second immature method of psychological defense is based on complaining, procrastinating, or setting bait for trouble. In this the combat veteran anticipates rejection, problems, and harm, and baits others to respond in an irritable and angry fashion. This allows the combat veteran to react in an angry manner.

As you work through an understanding of combat PTSD, you may ask yourself whether you are blaming, complaining, procrastinating or rather tilting at windmills or setting bait for trouble. These are defense mechanisms based on anger and a need for action. Knowing where a conflict resides provides a sense of focus. Understanding that this need for focus is a method of controlling anxiety, how can you transcend this need for blaming and complaining and find more productive methods of psychological defense to deal with your own quiet desperation?

Common (Neurotic) Methods Of
Psychologiacal Defense For Combat PTSD

We all have defense mechanisms. In psychology defense mechanism refers to techniques used to maintain a sense of self or self-worth. This concept of defense mechanisms was first developed by Sigmund Freud. In his psychoanalytic model of the mind, defense mechanisms were primarily for the defense of the ego. The ego refers to a sense of self or self-worth. For the combat veteran, these psychological defenses run deeper than that. More than just a method to maintain one's sense of integrity or self-worth, **defense mechanisms typically utilized are responsible for maintaining a sense of safety.** Self-worth, even self-esteem, are a luxury.

There are three primary methods of psychological defense mechanisms common for combat PTSD. These all arise from the fight/flight model of arousal. They include: 1) Command and Control; 2) Bunker Down; and 3) On the Road Again.

Command and control refers to the need by a combat veteran to control as much of his environment as is possible. If you are unable to control your perimeter and to maintain your environment this typically leads to feelings of anxiety. The defense mechanism of command and control leads the combat veteran to taking excessive steps to maintain his environment. This can become a compulsive feature. Many times a combat veteran will be seen by others as busy, fidgety, as well as bossy.

The second method of psychological defense for combat PTSD is referred to as Bunkering or Bunker Down. This refers to a tendency to isolate oneself from others. The combat veteran might have a favorite room, spot in the house, yard, or even within the immediate vicinity where he is able to be alone. When the combat veteran bunkers down, he is inaccessible to others. He may feel safe, but others might be irritable with the combat veteran because of his personal distance.

A third method of psychological defense for combat PTSD is referred to as On the Road Again. Many times a combat veteran will feel more comfortable if on the road or taking a short trip, going to the desert, mountains, or some other physical location away from the home in order to change one's environment. Movement away from perceived danger or difficulties is a method of psychological defense.

As you examine yourself and your own natural tendencies to maintain safety, what psychological defense mechanisms are you using to help you feel more comfortable? These defense mechanisms for safety are all deficiency mechanisms. These in of themselves are not the healthiest ways to handle emotional difficulty or perceived threat. However, by understanding these mechanisms and knowing that you are utilizing them because you feel threatened and have a need for safety can allow you to feel more comfortable by simply understanding the process.

What methods do you typically use and what have you done to educate your loved ones regarding your own needs for safety and how you can achieve that? Sometimes simply going to one's room or bunker for a period of time allows the veteran to have a sense of safety so that they can later rejoin the family and/or loved ones. At other times it is a matter of maintaining a sense of control and order. At other times, it is the need to take a long drive into the desert or to the mountains to just get away for a period of time. These fight/flight methods help the veteran find and experience safety.

Mature Psychological Defenses For Validation

The true nature of anything is what it becomes at its highest.

Aristotle

Psychological defense mechanisms for combat PTSD are conceived of as either immature, neurotic, or mature. At its highest level, these defense mechanisms are responsible in part for channeling angst and that underlying anxiety which permeates the veteran's life into activities which are productive and transcend the day-to-day mundane and trivial aspects of life.

While immature defenses are responsible for assisting the veteran maintain a sense of integrity and survival, and neurotic or common psychological defenses such as Command and Control, Bunker Down, and On the Road Again are necessary for safety, **mature psychological defenses provide an ongoing source of validation, and, once engaged, can become a compelling force directing one's life.**

Sublimation, or The Power of Piddling, the veteran puts his energy into productive and successful activities. This could include a hobby such as wood working, or taking care of one's garden. The essential point is that the veteran is involved in either creative or productive activities which maintain the environment, or rather contribute to a successful environment.

Another mature method of psychological defense comes from the **Healing Power of Helping Others. By assisting others who are in trouble and in need, who need direction, guidance, or someone to listen to, the veteran learns much about himself and gains mastery over more fundamental skills.**

William Glasser, M.D., a psychiatrist and proponent of reality therapy, describes two types of individuals: successful, and unsuccessful. Individuals who are sublimating their activities through the power of piddling or finding the healing power of helping are successful and they are contributing to ongoing social interactions of others. This provides a sense of validation, esteem, and self-worth.

The more primitive methods of defense can be considered unsuccessful methods. Immature methods are always unsuccessful methods of defense because they tear down ongoing productive relationships with others, undermining the basic tenants of our social network. Neurotic or common methods of psychological defense for combat PTSD can become unsuccessful if they lead to the undermining of the social core the veteran lives within.

What can you do as a veteran, understanding these methods of defense, to identify those common practices which are unsuccessful, and channel your energy into achieving safety through common methods of defense and when strength is found to contribute to successful interactions with others through the power of helping and creating?

Hierarchy Of Needs For Combat PTSD

Fear is the main souce of superstition,
and one of the main sources of cruelty.
To conquer fear is the beginning of wisdom.

Burtrand Russell

Maslow and other social psychologists have posited a hierarchy of needs which begin with basic or deficiency needs and are followed by being needs.

Defense mechanisms can be understood as falling within these needs beginning with deficiency needs and eventually passing through to mature defense mechanisms which are being needs. The transition then, follows unsuccessful activities which destroy or take down successful social relationships with others to productive defense strategies which enhance our relationships.

At the lowest level a deficiency need, but an ultimately necessary need, is the need for survival. This is characteristic of unsuccessful interpersonal strategies in that this does not generate productive social relationships. Immature psychological defense mechanisms such as blaming, complaining, and procrastinating are indicative of this need for survival.

The second need is safety and can either be a deficiency or being need, and either a successful or unsuccessful activity are those common and neurotic defense mechanisms which include Command and Control, Bunker Down, and On the Road Again.

A being need for combat PTSD is validation. This is a successful identity, a successful activity that transcends deficiency needs and it is accompanied by a sense of self-worth and a need for knowing.

What have you done to develop successful relationships among others and to encourage a successful relationship within your own primary and family relationships? How does focusing in on successful activities and being needs help you overcome your own fear, your own anger, and your own hatred?

Hierarchy of Needs for Combat PTSD

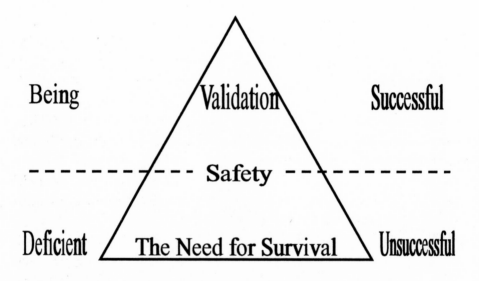

Fixation

Fixation refers to the arrest of psychosocial development. Fixation is a term that was first used by Sigmund Freud. Freud was trained as a neurologist and developed a model of the mind based on his understanding of electricity, hydraulics, and the nervous system. Freud was able to see that neurons communicated to the next neuron not through a steady electrical current, but a combination of electrical, chemical processes.

When looking at psychosexual development, he noted that children who had difficulty in certain areas, became fixated orally, anally, and psychosexually.

One of Freud's contemporaries, Ericson, was able to develop a model of social or psychosocial development. He noted that trauma can interfere with psychosexual, psychosocial development.

As a combat veteran, **you entered combat as either an adolescent still in the process of developing a personal identity or a young man who had already assumed a level of leadership.** Significant trauma leads to a fixation of one's development. In understanding this process, how are current abilities, aptitudes, interests, and ability to take responsibility or assume leadership been affected by your war time experiences?

Individuals who did not have leadership responsibility while in combat have difficulty assuming responsibility later on in life. There is a problem in accepting structure, a tendency to rebel against that structure, and also problems in developing interpersonal structure for oneself. Those who had positions of command and responsibility have a greater need for control, not only of themselves, but all aspects of their home and environment. In thinking about fixation and understanding that that is the natural process, how has the traumatic experience impacted you? and, what can you do to thwart the impact of such fixation?

Unfinished Business—
Setting Bait For Trouble
The High And Low Road
Coping Skills Bag Of Tricks

When people overreact to a moment, become too angry, too sad, too aggressive, too anxious, to a particular situation, it is most likely that the events of that moment have triggered unfinished business. Unfinished business occurs because of past life history or past trauma. There is a certain lack of closure, and because there is this lack of closure, an issue or event remains emotionally unresolved. These are stored as cognitions in your mind.

As combat veterans, you are aware of certain triggers, sights, and sounds, which can lead to an automatic level of arousal. Unfinished business may include triggers of conditioned stimuli, but these also refer to certain events. These can include: interacting with others who have strongly held opinions, being stuck in traffic, long lines at a supermarket, frustration finding items which have been misplaced around the home, and taking feelings out on loved ones around us.

As a combat veteran, it is most likely that there were events in your traumatic history which you did not have an opportunity to gain closure or mastery over. Because of this, certain events and triggers can arouse a heightened level of emotional response. You might take a moment to think through events in which you overreacted and see if there is any pattern. Does this pattern include times when you are exposed to large groups of people or feel confined? What do you do with this emotional response? Do you take the emotional response out on those whom are closest to you? Do you look for situations for an intense emotional response? Do you set yourself up for trouble?

We have discussed previously how a more primitive part of our brain can lead to an intense emotional response. We have also learned that this primitive part of the brain, primarily the amygdala, can learn to begin responding with fear and rage without involving the higher cortex. We have developed coping skills in order to reduce the likelihood that the low road, the dinosaur dump, will be taken, and instead the high road, utilizing our cerebral cortex can be incorporated in our response. **By utilizing our cerebral cortex, the smart brain, we can stop our stinkin' thinkin' and reframe and gain closure over those events that are likely to trigger unfinished business. Over a period of time you will learn, again, to take the high road rather than the low road.**

As you learn to master the symptoms of a post traumatic stress disorder, you gain an arsenal. What is in your bag of tricks to help you cope? We have discussed breathing techniques, visualization skills, cognitive skills to stop stinkin' thinkin' and we have also discussed gaining focus and mastery over the moment through awareness.

What is in your bag of tricks? What are your strengths in coping with your own unfinished business?

Survivor Guilt
The Grieving Process And Finding Closure

Scott Peck, M.D., a psychiatrist, wrote in his self-help book *A Road Less Traveled*, psychopathology or mental health problems can be divided into three basic types: psychosis, neurosis, and personality disorders. A psychosis occurs when an individual distorts reality. Psychotic individuals may hear voices and see things that aren't there, or believe the world is significantly different from the way it is. A neurosis is a condition which occurs when the individual takes on responsibility for more than they personally are truly responsible for. A personality disorder occurs when an individual has an inability or lacks the ability to accept personal accountability or culpability for their own bad acts.

A post traumatic stress disorder is a neurosis. One of the concomitants of this disorder is survivor guilt. **Frequently, combat veterans feel guilty about having survived their combat experience, and this affects their sense of self-esteem and self-worth.**

It is important to remember that **only good people feel guilty.** People who have personality disorders, who are psychopaths, or sociopaths have difficulty accepting personal responsibility for their own bad actions. A combat veteran may feel angry, bitter, and act on these impulses, yet a combat veteran typically will feel very bad for their own shortcomings or bad acts.

Have you ever found yourself feeling down because of your own behavior? Do you ever find yourself feeling guilty for your actions, and feeling guilty for having survived combat?

Ross, a psychologist who has studied the grieving process, discussed stages of grief. These include denial, bargaining, anger, depression, and acceptance. In a combat setting many times when comrades were lost, either wounded in action or killed in action, there wasn't time to grieve. Because casualties were taken away and replacements followed, it was very typical of a combatant to deal with their combat experience through a sense of denial, bargaining, and a low level of anger. When we experience loss, the first stage is typically denial which is characterized by feelings of shock and disbelief. This is often followed by a period of bargaining in which we view our own actions and actions of others, and replay the loss asking the question: What could I have done differently? When looking back at comrades lost in action or severely wounded, what statements do you make to yourself regarding actions you might have taken? How could you have acted differently? And if you did so, would that have made a difference?

Psychologists who study loss know that bargaining or replaying in one's mind different actions or scenarios that would have changed the outcome preventing the loss of a comrade is a way we play a trick on ourselves in order to keep someone still alive in our own mind. This can lead to our own stinkin'thinkin' regarding what we are, who we are, and the consequences of our own action on individuals lost in action.

There is an extreme level of anger regarding circumstances and situations that follows when we truly understand loss. You might want to ask yourself when you are feeling extremely angry: What types of self statements have you made, and have you engaged in the bargaining process? **We typically attempt to find blame for these extreme losses, and part of a post traumatic stress disorder is assuming guilt and responsibility for things which are truly beyond our own ability to** control. By accepting culpability we find one measure, a sense of closure, but the problem leaves us with a sense of being unworthy.

This sense of unworthiness can leave an individual feeling that they don't deserve to have a good life, to be loved, to be accepted by those around them. This sense of personal disrespect can significantly interfere with your ability to reach out and connect with others around you. You want to ask yourself how your own conclusions regarding your own self-worth interfere with your relationships with significant others—your wife, your children, your family, and close friends.

The problem then is in self acceptance. Working through the guilt realizing that survivor guilt is common, and a component of a post traumatic stress disorder can make it easier to find acceptance with oneself. It is important to confront those stinkin' thinkin' dialogues that interfere with your ability to respect yourself. When you feel guilty, remembering that only good people feel guilty is one method to find a sense of good grief moving towards acceptance thereby gaining closure.

How We Sleep—Nightmares— Sleep Apnea—Dream Innoculation Therapy—Sleep Induction Techniques

One of the most common complaints of combat veterans with combat post traumatic stress disorders is the problem of sleep. **Mechanisms of sleep are fairly well understood.** Typically, after we fall asleep our brain waves slow down until we are in a theta wave anywhere from four to eight cycles per second. After forty-five minutes of restful sleep REM sleep occurs, rapid eye movement, where we dream. When this happens, brain activity returns to a level that typically is observed during daytime activity. Why is this occurring? What impact does that have on a combat veteran?

Tucked below the cortex in the mid brain are structures in the hypothalamus which essentially act as a thermostat. When respiration slows to a critical level endocrine secretions trigger the reticular activating system, the generator in the brain located at the base or hind brain at the top of the spinal column, to release a burst of electricity. This burst of electricity travels up through the hind brain into the mid brain or dinosaur brain, as well have discussed, where this electricity passes through our thalamic relays into the auditory and visual areas of the cortex, the temporal and occipital lobes respectively. During this REM period the brain is experiencing the neurological activity that occurs during the day during wakeful periods.

Neural connections of auditory and visual information are synthesized by our frontal lobes and dreaming occurs. Typically, the self is not directly involved and one experiences a dream as happening around oneself rather than understanding that the mind is actually creating the ongoing dream.

Studies of combat veterans have shown that exposure to combat has a tendency to decrease the size of the hippocampus. The hippocampus is essentially the photocopier that forms auditory and visual information in memory. It is noted that in individuals who have lesions or any type of disturbance to their hippocampus that there is an impairment in sleep. Additionally, hippocampus difficulties are also associated with problems in memory and in irritability. Studies of combat veterans have shown that the hippocampus size decreases and, in comparison, the amygdala which is responsible for fight/flight and other aggressive responses increases, and fear responses have a tendency to override the smart brain or the cortex.

Our dreams are the result of electrical stimulation of specific areas of our cortex. In our cortex, our brain's DNA produces RNA. That RNA has been used not to replicate brain cells but rather to code memories through a series of amino acid changes. We store information categorically. During the day when we experience new things, new learning, or other experiences our neurons manufacture RNA which codes information for our learning. It is thought that dreaming is extremely important because it allows the brain to naturally organize and to sort information categorically, or to group into associations, and for combat veterans to assimilate this new learning into existing cognitions. When electricity forces through the mind into cognitions of previous learning that have been tripped or triggered by the day's events, this electricity runs from one cognition to a cognition that somehow is similarly or categorically related.

Nightmares are believed to occur more frequently for combat veterans particularly because the hippocampus which is responsible for holding information in memory is less effective and the amyglada becomes involved. With that, feelings of terror and panic can become incorporated in one's dreams.

Nightmares then ensue and when the amygdala is stimulated it results in a series of endocrine functions that ultimately lead to production of adrenaline. Adrenaline, when it is released into the body becomes a neurochemical transmitter inside the brain, primarily norepinephrine and epinephrine. Consequently, nightmares can lead to night terrors, and with this a full blown adrenaline dump can occur.

Combat veterans are frequently diagnosed with sleep apnea. Sleep apnea is believed primarily to be a consequence of difficulty breathing. Combat veterans have a tendency to not breath when they are under stress. This occurs because it is a natural defense that the body utilizes in order to help manufacture adrenaline. While dreaming, particularly if a nightmare is occurring, breathing can stop and adrenaline ends up being manufactured. A combat veteran may wake in a startle and have a full blown arousal reaction as a result of a horrific or terrible dream.

What can be done to improve sleeping involves behavioral interventions as well as medical interventions. These sleep problems appear to be chronic and require ongoing management. **First it is important to understand that use of deep breathing relaxation techniques prior to sleep can be helpful to ensure healthier sleep patterns. Another technique involves dream inoculation therapy.** Just before dozing off when entering a level of relaxation following use of deep breathing exercises, it is possible to tell oneself that if I do dream I will recognize that I am in a dream and I will be able to change the outcome of the dream.

This requires some regular and repetitive practice. It is necessary to do this because you are depending on the random electrical activity in the brain to eventually trigger the self. Once this occurs, it is more common that it will occur again in the future and the self can become involved in dampening a horrific dream.

Sleep apnea is frequently treated with a breathing machine, and these increase the comfort a veteran will feel throughout the night. Dreaming is reported to increase while utilizing the breathing machine. The best thing about such machines is that they help prevent a wild ride or dinosaur dump which ensues after an individual holds their breath while dreaming.

There are also medications that are available to improve sleep. Available at health food stores is the valerian root. This has been shown to assist in sleeping. Tricyclic medications such as trazodone and doxepin are helpful and other serotonin re-uptake inhibitors such as paxil, zoloft and prozac have also been shown to be very helpful in increasing sleep patterns.

The serotonin re-uptake inhibitors such as paxil, zoloft and prozac allow for the build up of serotonin. When a certain level of serotonin is reached you feel sleepy and fall asleep. Serotonin is thought to be manufactured during the day when we are in an alert and restful waking state. Other natural neurochemicals are manufactured when we are in a restful sleep. The tricyclic medications such as elavil, doxepin, and trazodone deal more with neurochemicals such as dopamine acetylcholine which are thought to be manufactured during the night when we are having a restful sleep period.

What techniques have you found to help you sleep? What triggers are you aware of that seem to set off nightmares or other sleep disturbances. When you are having difficulty sleeping, rather than spend your time tossing and turning in bed it would be more helpful to get up for a period of time, perhaps go outside and take a half-dozen deep breaths or read and watch television until you begin to feel sleepy. It is not helpful to toss and turn in bed all night if you are not able to sleep. Many times these difficulties as well as waking in terror can be disturbing to the sleep of your significant other. Explaining this relationship to loved ones is helpful in reducing anxiety veterans typically have regarding sleep.

Secondary Wounding, Indignation, And Secondary PTSD

Secondary Wounding is a common difficulty which combat veterans face who have PTSD. In order to have **Secondary Wounding** it is necessary first to have been traumatized in the first place and have unfinished business from a previous past trauma. As a warrior, you were so exposed. **Secondary Wounding** occurs when you are reminded of your wartime experience and trauma, and that experience is not validated by significant others around you—family members, friends, acquaintances, people you don't know, or society in general. One World War II Pacific Theater veteran described attempting to share with his eldest son his experiences in combat, however briefly, and to relate how those memories remain quite painful. Much to this veteran's disappointment this gentleman's son responded: "Dad, can't you get over that? The war was over fifty years ago." Vietnam veterans often feel this lack of validation and wounding for being part of a war which was not won. Korean veterans report that they were told that they were not in a war, but rather a police action or a conflict. A common theme running throughout, is this lack of validation for one's experience.

This lack of validation often leads to feelings of Indignation. Indignation is the type of anger which occurs when an individual feels that others around them are less than grateful. This ingratitude is seen as an injustice, and one's effort as a warrior or as a combatant seems small if not meaningless. **Indignation is a righteous anger that boils from this lack of validation.**

For most combat veterans anger is a common difficulty. This lack of validation gives rise to an edge and more than this, **Indignation.** This is presented to others as scorn and anger. This **Indignation**, the edge, the scorn, and anger, and can cause harm to those significant others around us resulting in **Secondary Post Traumatic Stress Disorders.**

People who work with, live with, interact with persons with post traumatic stress disorders can develop **Secondary PTSD.** Though not yet listed in *the Diagnostic Statistical Manuel of Mental Health Disorders*, it is more than likely to soon be in forthcoming editions. The essential sequela of **Secondary PTSD** are common characteristics with other types of PTSD including hypervigilance and a marked startle reaction, intrusive memories, as well as an expectation for harm, and anger. But **Secondary PTSD** differs from combat PTSD with the absence of actual exposure to the horror of combat.

How can you as a veteran learn to identify your own **Indignation.** How can you let go of this scorn when you feel less than validated and avoid developing any sense of a righteous anger looking for payback and retribution? What can you do to prepare your significant others for your anger? What steps can you take to find a clear space and a safe space in order to let go of this anger?

Afterword

◆

AT EASE

*Be as one with all creation,
in beauty, in harmony, and in peace,
and may you walk your own road with a cool body.*

R. Carlos Nakai

The preceding essays have been designed to assist you as a combat veteran in developing a more comprehensive understanding of your own inner self and the world which you live in; for there are two worlds: The physical world around you, the one that you sense, see, touch, taste, smell, and share with others, and the world within yourself.

The self as we have seen is a central character in a cast of players. The one held ultimately responsible for yourself is the central character who has the ability to act and change in a moment. We in ourselves can grow, understand, and accommodate.

At Ease: We live on oxygen. By learning to breathe, learning to monitor our triggers, our cues, by learning coping skills, your bag of tricks, you have reached this point in this journey, hopefully, with a better understanding of these two worlds.

There is the world outside of you, and the world within that carries with you memories of wartime experience, and what for others has been, but for you continues as fresh and as vivid as this moment and the next.

Through these essays you have developed an inner voice that has come to understand both the outer world and your inner self.

So you live in two worlds. With harmonic balance, there is essential well being, validation, even joy.

At Ease.

References

———— ◆ ————

Anderson, J.R. (1983). *The architecture of cognition*. Cambridge, MA: Harvard University Press.

Topic: Spreading Activation

Baudura, A., & Walters, R. (1963). *Social learning and personality development*. New York: Holt, Rinehart & Winston.

Topic: Frustration—Aggression Hypothesis: Social Learning of Aggression

Becker, E. (1973). *The denial of death*. New York: The Free Press

Berliner, L. & Briere, J. Trauma, memory, and clinical practice. In L. Williams (Ed). *Trauma and memory*. Thousand Oaks, CA: Sage.

Briere, J. (1997). *Psychological assessment of adult posttraumatic states*. Washington P.C.: American Psychological Association.

Buss, D.M. (1999). *Evolutionary psychology: The new science of the mind*. Boston: Allyn and Bacon.

Carlson, E.B. (1997). *Trauma assessments: A clinician's guide*. The Guilford Press, New York: The Guilford Press.

Carlson, N.R. (1999). *Foundations of physiological psychology—4th ed.* Boston: Allyn and Bacon.

Carter-Scott, C., (1998). *If life is a game, these are the rules.* New York: Broadway Books.

Charney, D.S., Deutch, A.Y., Krystal, J.H., Soothwich, S.M., & Davis, M. (1993). Psychobiologic mechanisms of post-traumatic stress disorder. *Archives of General Psychiatry,* 50, 294-305.

Collins, A.M., & Loftus, E.F. (1975). A spreading—activation theory of semantic processing. *Psychological Review,* 82, 407-428.

Topic: Spreading Activation

Da Costa, J.M. (1871). On irritable heart: a clinical study of a form of functional cardiac disorder and its consequence. *American Journal of Medical Science.* 61:17.

Topic: Battle Heart

Duorclak, R.J. (ed). (19993). *Battle for Korea: The Associated Press history of the Korean conflict.* Pennsylvania: Combined Books.

Follette, V.M., Ruzek, J.F., & Abueg, F.R.. (Eds). (1998). *Cognitive behavioral therapies for trauma.* New York: The Guilford Press.

Topic: Cognitive Behavior Theories

Ford, N. (1994). *The sleep rx: 75 proven ways to get a good night's sleep.* Englewood Cliffs, New Jersey: Prentice Hall.

Glasser, W. (1989). *Reality therapy: a new approach to psychotherapy.* New York: Harper Collins

Golderberg, H. (1976). *The hazards of being male.* Greta, La.: Wellness Institute

Guruitz, T.V., Shenton, M.E., & Pitman, R.K. (1995). Reduced hippocampal volume on magnetic resonance imaging in chronic post-traumatic stress disorder. *Paper presented at the annual meeting of the International Society for Traumatic Stress Studies, Miami.*

Heegan, J. (ed). (1994). *The Times Atlas of the Second World War.* New York: Cresent Books.

Howard, P.J. (1999). *The owner's manual for the brain: Everyday applications from mind-brain research—2nd* ed. Austin, Texas: Band Press.

Janoff-Bulman, R. (1992). *Shattered assumptions: Toward a new psychology of trauma.* New York: Free Press.

Topic: Shattered Assumptions

Joseph, R. (1988). Dual mental functioning in a split-brain patient. *Journal of Clinical Psychology,* 44(5), 770-779.

Krystal, J.H., Bennett, A., Bremner, D., Southwick, S.M., & Charney, D.S. (1996). Recent developments in the neurobiology of dissociation. In L.K. Michelson & W.J. Rax (Eds.), *Handbook of dissociation: Theoretical, empirical, and clinical perspectives* (pp. 163-190). New York: Plenum.

Kubler-Ross, E. (1997). *On death and dying.* New York: Simon & Schuster.

Kulka, R.A., Schlenger, W.E., Fairbank, J.A., Hough, R.L., Jordan, B.K., Marmau, C.R., Weiss, D.S. & Grady, D.A. (1990). *Trauma and the iet-nam War Generation: Report of Findings from the National Vietnam Veterans Readjustment Study.* Levitown, PA: Bronner/Mazel.

Leahey, T.H., & Harris, R.J. (1997). *Learning and Cognition* (4ed). Upper Saddle River, New Jersey: Prentice-Hall, Inc.

Leakey, R., & Lewin, R. (1992). *Origins reconsidered: In search of what makes us human.* New York: Doubleday.

Le Doux, J. (1998). *The emotional brain: The mysterious underpinnings of emotional life.* New York: Touchstone.

Macleod, A.D. (1991). Posttraumatic stress disorder in world war II vet-erans. *New Zealand Medical Journal.* 104: 285-288.

Topic: WWII veteran's adjustment problems increased after retirement

Matsakis, A. (1996). *I can't get over it: A handbook for trauma survivors* (2ed). Oakland, California: New Harbinger Publications, Inc.

McCorath, E.L. *The complete idiot's guide to beating the blues.* New York: Alpha Books.

Parrish, I.S. (1999). *Military veterans ptsd reference manual.* Bryn Mawr, PA: Buy Books on The Web.com.

Topic: How to seek compensation

Pechura, C.M., & Rall, D.P. (Eds). (1993). *Veterans at risk: the health effects of mustard and lewisite.* Washington, D.C.: National Academy Press.

Peck, M.S. (1998). *The road less traveled.* New York: Trade Paperback.

Piaget, J. (1997). *The essential Piaget.* (H.E. Guber and J.J. Vaneche, Eds.) New York: Basic Books.

Sagan, C. (1994). *Pale blue dot: A vision of the human future in space.* New York: Random House.

Sapolsky, R.M. Hideo, E., Rebert, C.S., & Finch, C.E. (1990). Hippocampal damage associated with prolonged glucocorticoid exposure in primates. *Journal of Neuroscience*, 10, 2897-2902.

Seligman, M. (1975). *Helplessness: On depression development and death.* San Francisco: W.H. Freeman.

Topic: Learned Helplessness

Seligman, M.E.P. (1991). *Learned optimism.* New York: Knof.

Shapiro, F. (1995). *Eye movement desensitization and reprocessing: Basic principles, protocols, and procedures.* New York: Guilford Press.

Topic: EMDR

Skinner, B.F. (1972). *Beyond freedom and dignity.* New York: Bantam.

Topic: Operant Conditioning, conditioned Stimulus, learning theory

Stanton, S.L. (1985). *The rise and fall of an American Army.* Novato, Ca.: Presidio Press.

Summers, J.W.G. (1995). *Historical atlas of the Vietnam War.* New York: Houghton Mifflin Company.

Vander Kolk, B.A. (1994). The body keeps the score: Memory and the evolving psychobiology of PTSD. *Harvard Review of Psychiatry,* 1, 253-265.

Vander Kolk, B.A., McFarlane, A.C. & Lar Weisaeth, Eds. (1996). *Traumatic stress: The effects of overwhelming experience on mind, body, and society.* New York: The Guilford Press.

Wagner, A.M., & Lineham, M.M. (1998). *Dissociative behavior.* In V.M. Follette, J.II. Ruzek, & F.R. Abueg (Eds.), Cognitive behavioral therapies for trauma. (pp. 191-225). New York: The Guilford Press.

Topic: Dissociation

Wilson, E.O. (1998). *Consilience: The unity of knowledge.* New York: Alfred A. Knopf.

Weil, A. (1998). *Natural health, natural medicine.* Boston; New York: Houghton Mifflin Company.

Wright, R. (1994). *The moral animal: The new science of evolutionary psychology.* New York: Vintase Books.

Printed in the United States
36255LVS00005B/99